The Software
Challenge

Other Publications:
WEIGHT WATCHERS® SMART CHOICE RECIPE COLLECTION
TRUE CRIME
THE AMERICAN INDIANS
THE ART OF WOODWORKING
LOST CIVILIZATIONS
ECHOES OF GLORY
THE NEW FACE OF WAR
HOW THINGS WORK
WINGS OF WAR
CREATIVE EVERYDAY COOKING
COLLECTOR'S LIBRARY OF THE UNKNOWN
CLASSICS OF WORLD WAR II
TIME-LIFE LIBRARY OF CURIOUS AND UNUSUAL FACTS
AMERICAN COUNTRY
VOYAGE THROUGH THE UNIVERSE
THE THIRD REICH
THE TIME-LIFE GARDENER'S GUIDE
MYSTERIES OF THE UNKNOWN
TIME FRAME
FIX IT YOURSELF
FITNESS, HEALTH & NUTRITION
SUCCESSFUL PARENTING
HEALTHY HOME COOKING
LIBRARY OF NATIONS
THE ENCHANTED WORLD
THE KODAK LIBRARY OF CREATIVE PHOTOGRAPHY
GREAT MEALS IN MINUTES
THE CIVIL WAR
PLANET EARTH
COLLECTOR'S LIBRARY OF THE CIVIL WAR
THE EPIC OF FLIGHT
THE GOOD COOK
WORLD WAR II
HOME REPAIR AND IMPROVEMENT
THE OLD WEST

This volume is one of a series that examines
various aspects of computer technology and
the role computers play in modern life.

The Software Challenge

BY THE EDITORS OF TIME-LIFE BOOKS

TIME-LIFE BOOKS, ALEXANDRIA, VIRGINIA

Contents

Test Flights for Software

Just as the space shuttle *Columbia* was about to begin her maiden voyage, the countdown was abruptly halted when the spacecraft's onboard computers and those at Mission Control in Houston disagreed by a few milliseconds on how far the launch procedure had progressed. Analysts quickly discovered that changes made in the shuttle's software over years of development had introduced a one in sixty-seven chance that the two computer systems would be out of sync when they were turned on for the mission.

Columbia's aborted launch embodies all the frustrations that attend the creation of complex computer programs. The intricately woven cloth of logic seems never to be quite finished or quite correct. Features fail to function according to plan, or they may simply be missing. Additional capabilities are frequently called for when the software is all but complete. Each of these circumstances occasions changes that are almost as likely to introduce new faults as they are to remedy existing ones.

Programmers strive mightily to get computer software right the first time, but doing so has been an elusive goal except for the simplest of jobs. More than in any other human edifice, the sequences of instructions that constitute computer software are unforgiving of flaws in their construction. Compared to mechanical structures such as bridges and buildings, which adapt to small amounts of unexpected stress, computer programs are brittle. Instead of bending, they break.

Logical inconsistencies in a program's design, which often seem obvious when they are discovered, are one form of brittleness. For example, specifications for a section of a program intended to process elementary-school enrollments might stipulate that a child must be six years old before October 15 in order to enter the first grade. But another section of the program, designed perhaps by a different team, might require only that a child have completed kindergarten to be qualified for elementary school. In this situation, parents of a youngster born on November 1 might receive a notice of enrollment, only to find their child's name missing from the list of pupils that the school is expecting.

A mistake in computer-language grammar, such as a "/" inadvertently substituted for a "\" or some other seemingly minor error, can send a program off in a direction never anticipated, almost always with unpleasant consequences. Memory allocated to a particular function by one programmer, then reserved for another purpose by a different programmer, all but guarantees that the software will come to an ignominious halt sooner or later.

To exterminate bugs before they can cause disaster, software engineers rely on a variety of testing procedures, none of them foolproof. Software testing—known as validation—begins before a large program is assembled from its many pieces, each written as a separate program by different programmers in order to speed production.

As described on the following pages for hypothetical insurance-company software, validation generally proceeds in three stages. The first, called functional testing, is concerned with the accuracy of the results, or output, a program generates. Structural testing, the second stage, tests the consistency of a program's inner workings. Finally, after the program is assembled from its parts, critical program functions are checked to see that they work together as well as they functioned separately.

The more dreadful the consequences of software failure, of course, the more exhaustively a program is scrutinized before use. But large programs are called on to handle so vast a range of data and so many special cases that there is never enough time and money to test every conceivable circumstance of use. The validation process assures that a computer program is as sound as it can reasonably be—not that it is perfect.

Testing a Typical Sample

An automobile-insurance company's account-management programs must process vast amounts of data that is unique to each of its clients—name and address, sex, age, number of previous accidents, miles driven annually, and premiums, to mention just a few of the details. The values assigned to each of these particulars in the insurer's data base can reasonably be expected to fall within limits. The list of zip codes, for example, is finite in number. No insured driver can be younger than the minimum age required by law—or much more than 100 years old.

Ascertaining whether a program can handle the range of information that it will encounter is called boundary analysis. An aspect of functional testing, boundary analysis is one of the first trials that a program must pass on the road to validation. Programmers typically specify, in the software they write, a range of values for each item of information, or variable. To conduct a boundary analysis, a programmer tests the programs on the upper and lower ends of the range. Then a selection of intermediate values is tested. Few samples are needed if the range of values, such as dollar amounts of premiums, has no gaps. For zip codes, more examples should be tested to prove that the program rejects false values.

The software passes boundary analysis if it works as intended for all the values tested. Passing this milestone is no guarantee that a program will handle every value in a range, yet the chances are small that an untested value will cause difficulties if none of its neighbors have. For that reason, programmers accept a thoughtfully conducted boundary analysis as satisfactory evidence that all is as it should be with this aspect of the software.

Testing the limits. Represented by an army of figures, clients of a car-insurance company stand with their annual premiums emblazoned across their chests. Arrayed as a test for the program that will manage their policies are five drivers whose premiums span the entire range of values established by programmers for this variable, beginning with the lowest on the left and extending to the highest on the right. To pass boundary analysis, the program must demonstrate that it can flawlessly handle the full gamut of values.

Snares for
gram

ndary analysis, a program must next show
d to unusual combinations of values—as
outside the ranges that have been estab-
urching to a halt, or crashing. This second
nation is known as testing special cases.
equipped to handle these occurrences, the
k at such data.
ould be able to handle exceptions to gen-
ough most states do not permit the licens-
rounger than sixteen, the program must be

able to accept fifteen-year-olds from the few states that allow
them to drive. Coincidences—two drivers with identical
names and premiums, for example, or one driver with two
premiums because of owning two automobiles—also make
good special cases to test.

"Illegal values," that is, ones that fall outside the bound-
aries established for the software, also are fed into the program. Although there is no need for the software to process
this kind of information, which can arise from a misaimed
finger when information is first entered into the computer or
from the alteration of data in a memory bank as a result of a
temporary power loss, a program must not crash when presented with it. To pass this test, software must recognize
illegal values for what they are and pause while the information is corrected.

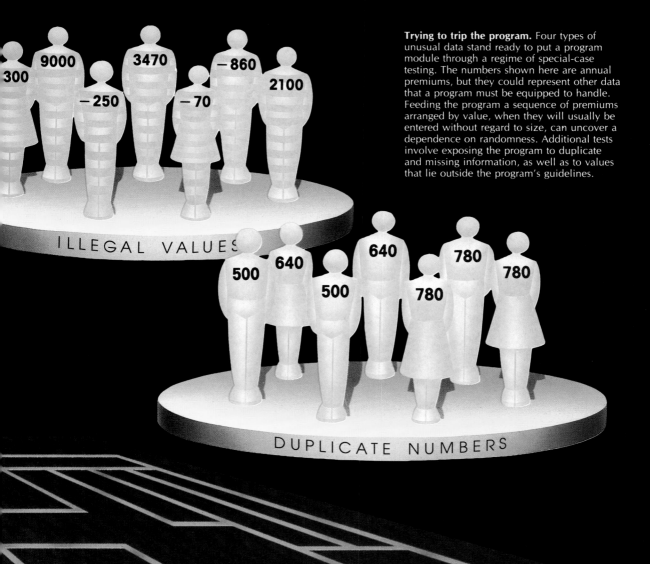

Trying to trip the program. Four types of
unusual data stand ready to put a program
module through a regime of special-case
testing. The numbers shown here are annual
premiums, but they could represent other data
that a program must be equipped to handle.
Feeding the program a sequence of premiums
arranged by value, when they will usually be
entered without regard to size, can uncover a
dependence on randomness. Additional tests
involve exposing the program to duplicate
and missing information, as well as to values
that lie outside the program's guidelines.

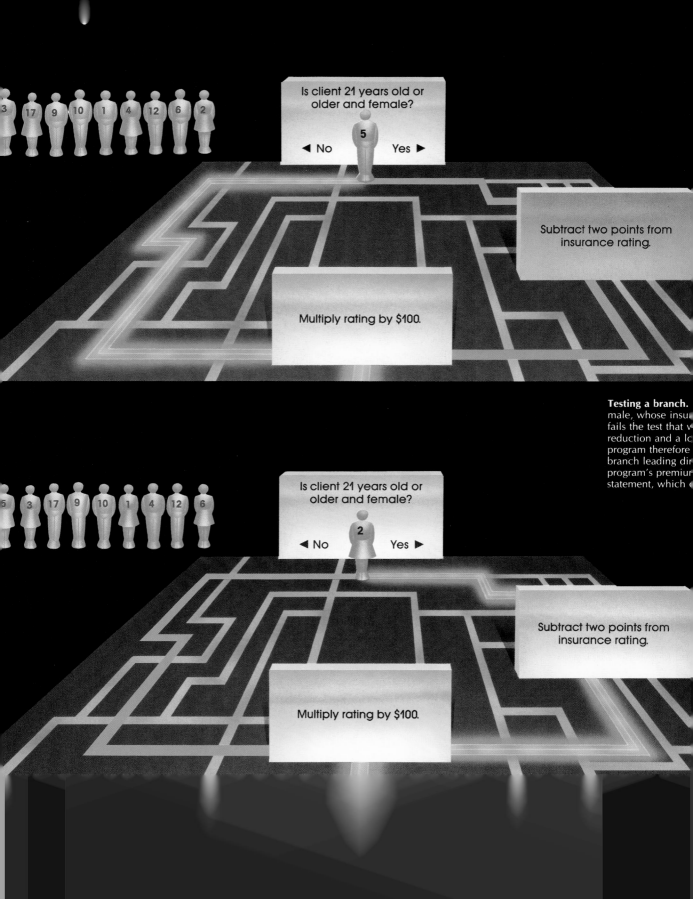

Is client 21 years old or older and female?

◄ No   **5**   Yes ►

Subtract two points from insurance rating.

Multiply rating by $100.

Testing a branch.
male, whose insu
fails the test that v
reduction and a lc
program therefore
branch leading dir
program's premiur
statement, which

Is client 21 years old or older and female?

◄ No   **2**   Yes ►

Subtract two points from insurance rating.

Multiply rating by $100.

Exploring a Program's Every Path

After functional testing is completed, each module of a large software package undergoes a second battery of examinations called structural testing. The objective is to probe each of the many convolutions within a complicated program.

Computer software consists largely of sequences of simple instructions linked by statements that compare data against specified criteria and then turn the program in one direction or another. For example, numbers larger than 100 might take the right fork in the program, while numbers equal to or smaller than 100 might diverge to the left.

One aspect of structural testing seeks to try the program with data that will exercise every branch. An important objective of such an examination is to ensure that data is passed to various branches as intended by the program's designers. Other goals are to determine whether each branch functions according to plan, to uncover any inconsistencies in the logic of the software, and to explore for any unintended branches in the program.

In the example shown on these pages, a conditional statement at the beginning of a program module divides drivers into two groups. Those who pose the smaller risk take a fork in the module that reduces their premiums; all others follow a path that leads to no reduction. As testing reveals, the rule for lowering premiums requires adjustment so that the program will charge no driver less than the company's $200 minimum premium.

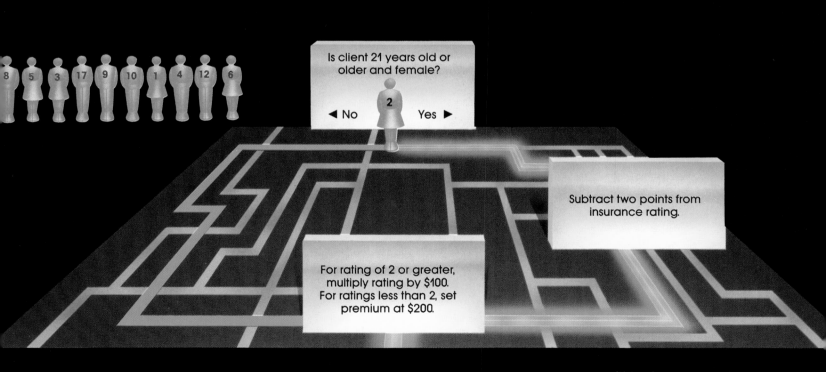

Is client 21 years old or older and female?

◄ No   2   Yes ►

Subtract two points from insurance rating.

For rating of 2 or greater, multiply rating by $100. For ratings less than 2, set premium at $200.

8 5 3 17 9 10 1 4 12 6

Modifying the program. To be certain that no female driver pays less than the $200 minimum, programmers modify the rule that calculates premiums so that it considers the insurance rating before doing the arithmetic.

Touring the Loops

A second aspect of structural testing is the examination of what are known as a program's loops. Any branch of a program may contain one or more loops, sets of instructions that a program performs repeatedly until specified conditions are met. A program might have a loop for dividing items into lots of ten. In effect, it would tell the computer to begin a lot, add items one at a time until there are ten, then open a new lot and repeat the process until there are no unassigned items.

A shortage of memory. The loop illustrated at right classifies clients as high or low risk and stores their files in separate areas of the computer's memory—a small space for low-risk drivers (they are comparatively rare) and a larger one for high-risk drivers. Alex, the client under review, has just been placed in the low-risk category, filling up the memory allocated to that group. Out of memory for low-risk customers, the program will crash when the next one comes along.

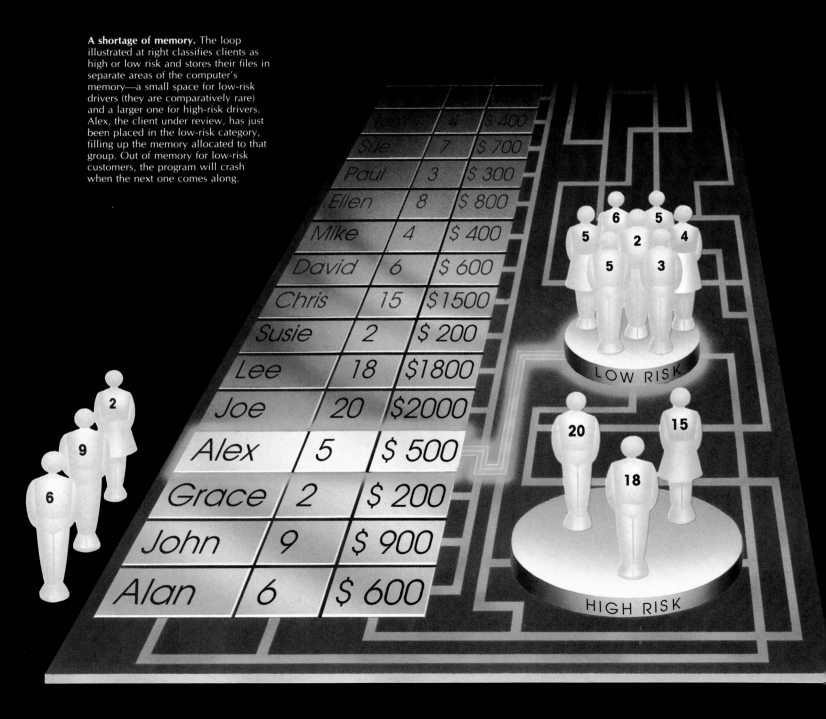

John	4	$ 400
Sue	7	$ 700
Paul	3	$ 300
Ellen	8	$ 800
Mike	4	$ 400
David	6	$ 600
Chris	15	$1500
Susie	2	$ 200
Lee	18	$1800
Joe	20	$2000
Alex	5	$ 500
Grace	2	$ 200
John	9	$ 900
Alan	6	$ 600

LOW RISK

HIGH RISK

Although the preceding example—and the one shown on these pages—are simple loops, large computer programs inevitably have many loops of great complexity. Furthermore, a loop in one branch may affect a loop in another, seemingly unrelated, pathway. And because loops may repeat an operation thousands of times without pause, executing these instructions can sometimes overload a computer's memory with data or in some other way cause the machine to crash.

These characteristics make testing loops the most uncertai aspect of validating software. Programmers typically test eac loop at least twice with different sets of information. Thi exposes faulty logic in a loop or reveals other programmin errors, such as insufficient memory *(left)*, that might caus difficulties soon after the software is placed in service. But th procedure offers no assurance that some future combinatio or mass of data will not expose an unsuspected flaw.

Correcting the fault. Programmers rewrite the software to reserve more memory for low-risk drivers, a simple matter in a computer big enough, as this one is, to give one category more memory without taking it from the other. However, should the ratio of low-risk drivers to high-risk drivers change, or should the program attempt to process an exceptionally long list of customers, the data could still overflow the allocated memory and cause the program to crash.

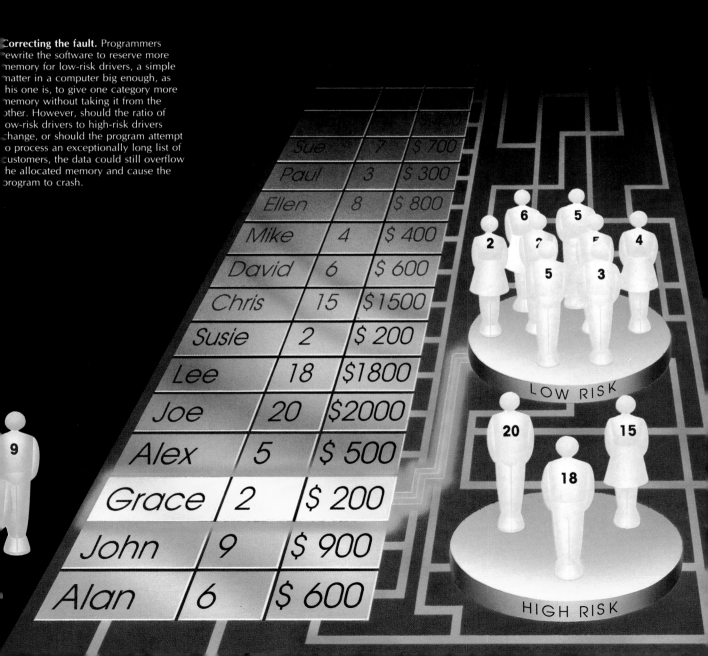

Sue	7	$ 700
Paul	3	$ 300
Ellen	8	$ 800
Mike	4	$ 400
David	6	$ 600
Chris	15	$1500
Susie	2	$ 200
Lee	18	$1800
Joe	20	$2000
Alex	5	$ 500
Grace	2	$ 200
John	9	$ 900
Alan	6	$ 600

LOW RISK

HIGH RISK

Verifying the Software Ensemble

After a program's individual modules have passed functional and structural muster, the pieces are assembled and the software tested as a whole. This stage of testing would be unnecessary if each segment of a program could be guaranteed faultless. According to the mathematics governing probabilities, if each piece of a complicated program is 100 percent reliable, then the combined parts will operate in flawless harmony. But if there is a mere one percent likelihood of error in each segment of, say, a ten-module program—a very high degree of reliability in the realm of computer software—the trustworthiness of the whole falls to 90 percent. If each module can be only 95 percent dependable, overall reliability plummets to 60 percent.

Thorough testing of the assembled modules is thus clearly desirable, yet it rarely occurs; there are simply too many routes through the software for all of them to be examined (right). So software designers employ a variety of strategies to ensure that a program works satisfactorily most of the time. Simple programs can be checked line by line, much as a proofreader would pore over a manuscript before publication. In the case of obviously critical pathways through large programs, humans are assigned to perform the same calculations as the software. Results are then compared and the causes of discrepancies ferreted out.

For computer programs that simply cannot be allowed to fail, there is a technique called N-version programming (below). Despite such measures, however, no complicated computer software—even programs that play crucial roles—can be exposed during testing to every conceivable situation it may encounter in actual use.

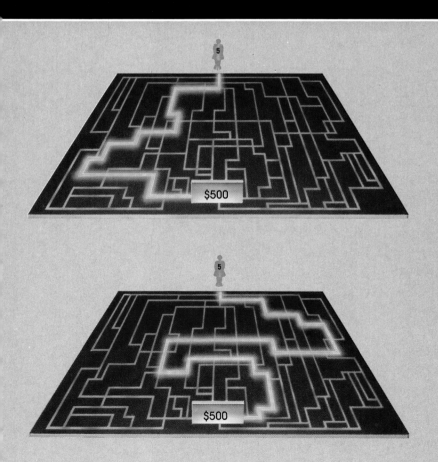

When Cost Is No Object

Two teams of programmers working independently are unlikely to make identical errors in writing software to a shared set of specifications. Thus, if the finished products yield indistinguishable results from a common set of data, both programs are probably correct. This principle stands behind N-version programming, a powerful method of validating complex software. Although N-version programming, combined with other testing methods, comes close to guaranteeing a bug-free program, the practice has several disadvantages. If the programs fail to agree, there is no simple way to tell which is at fault. Furthermore, drawing up a second program doubles development costs. Because of the expense of writing the programs and the difficulty of tracking down errors, N-version programming is reserved for software that must be as nearly perfect as possible—for example, programs that monitor patients in hospital intensive-care units, or those that control networks of automatic teller machines at banks.

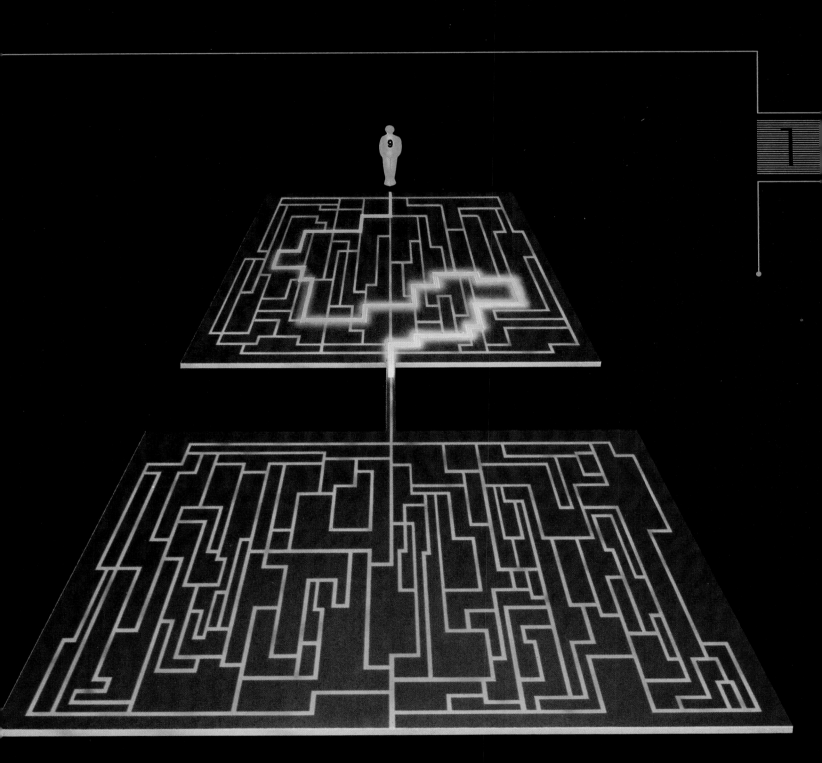

Proliferating pathways. Linking software
modules together makes a whole that is less
trustworthy than its parts. In the simple
example above, each module has just three
routes through it. Linking, however, triples the
number. Adding a third section would raise
the number of pathways to twenty-seven. If
each module had six paths, the total would
be 216, and thoroughly testing a program of
ten such modules would require examining
each of more than 60 million pathways.

Everests
of Complexity

The word software has been in widespread use since about 1960, when programs were first sold separately from the computer hardware on which they ran. Implying a malleability lacking in the machines themselves, the term refers to the instructions that tell computers what to do. The replacement of one set of instructions by another can produce protean changes, turning a tool for analyzing stock-market trends into a word processor, or an architect's electronic sketch pad into the control panel for an entire factory. Without detailed orders from a program, a computer can do nothing at all.

Sometimes software is a palpable presence—as in bank-teller machines, video games, or bar-code scanners at the supermarket checkout counter. At other times, it works subtly—in the machinery of elevators and medical instruments, in the dashboards of cars and the boxes that regulate traffic signals, in the casings of cameras, watches, food processors, and hair dryers. Whether sensed or not, it is everywhere. The industry that provides programs for the computers that pervade modern civilization ranks—like the hardware business—among the fastest growing in history.

Applications of software are plentiful, but so are the obstacles to making it. The slowness and labor-intensive nature of programming have been described as a crisis since the early 1950s. The alarm was first raised over the impracticality of addressing computers entirely in their native dialect of ones and zeros, known as machine language. The response, in the decades that followed, was a slew of so-called high-level languages—such as FORTRAN and COBOL—that allowed programmers to express their instructions in a more natural, English-like way. In spite of these advances, the sense of urgency about finding ways to produce software more quickly and reliably continued unabated through the 1960s and 1970s, particularly in the halls of the Pentagon, where programs were commissioned by the thousands. By all accounts, the crisis continues to this day. The Defense Science Board, a civilian advisory panel, states the software problem simply: "We cannot get enough of it to meet the demands of weapons-systems designers and users."

The Pentagon and the defense industry are not alone in these concerns. Banks, insurance companies, law firms, communications companies, universities, and any number of other institutions find themselves with backlogs of programming tasks that sometimes stretch as much as four to seven years into the future. Even traditionally low-tech industries, such as food processing, do not seem to be immune. The typical software package used to monitor operations in these and other businesses now requires something on the order of 30,000 programmer workdays to complete.

In spite of all this, demand for new software continues to intensify. Spending on programming in the United States increases annually at a rate of about 12 percent. The population of professional programmers worldwide, which numbered in the vicinity of three million in the early 1980s, now approaches eight million. Output has increased accordingly: In 1983, professional programming firms sold 6.5 billion lines of computer code. Today, the annual total is more than double that amount.

The sheer bulk of the programming load and the ever-rising expectations of computer users (inflated by the rapid pace of advances in hardware technology), have left the software industry struggling to keep up. For all the contributions of software to society—in accelerating the pace of scientific research, in making business more efficient and daily life more convenient—it remains the single greatest restraint on widening the use of computers. Nor is an insufficiency of software the only problem. The programming industry is also beset by complaints about quality. According to David A. Fisher, a computer scientist who has studied the software acquisition problems of the U.S. Department of Defense: "The symptoms appear in the form of software that is nonresponsive to user needs, unreliable, excessively expensive, untimely, inflexible, difficult to maintain, and not reusable." Many computer scientists fear that the problems will only get worse as the hardware advances from machines that funnel all their work through a single central processing unit—as do most computers today—to systems that divide up the tasks and do the processing with multiple CPU's.

The severity of the software logjam has spawned much research aimed at making computer programming a more productive and predictable pursuit. Dozens of potential solutions are proposed each year. They include ever more expressive languages, such as Pascal, C, and Ada; management tools for projecting schedules and costs in the development projects; and powerful work stations that put computer assistance at the fingertips of programmers. A number of these experimental solutions have shown positive results and have been adopted by the majority of programmers. But all of the developments to date have been, at best, partial solutions. So far, there is no panacea. Many computer scientists, including a few of the recognized pioneers of programming, such as FORTRAN collaborator John Backus, have abandoned the search for a cure-all within the framework of traditional software engineering. They are developing languages based on imaginative new models for programming. A few of these languages, such as Smalltalk, C++, and Simula, which embody an approach called object-oriented programming, are attracting adherents from the ranks of day-to-day project managers. But in the main, most programming is still produced the way it has been for years: It is hammered out, tested, debugged, and retested at a pace of roughly two lines of code per hour.

A FRAGMENTED INDUSTRY

Right from the start, the industry that materialized to compete for profits in computer programming has been a rather topsy-turvy affair. Of the approximately 25,000 software companies now operating in the United States, virtually none existed prior to the early 1960s. During its brief history, the industry has passed through two distinct phases. At first, the customers for software were limited primarily to governments and large corporations, which were the only institutions prosperous enough to lease the ponderous mainframes of the day. Like the hardware, the software was generally leased rather than bought, and the programming was not notable for great variety. Computing time was so expensive that it was reserved primarily for vital business functions such as accounting, inventory, and payroll. The companies producing the software—sizable firms such as Honeywell, ADP, and Sperry Rand—competed not so much on the merits of their finished programs as on the quality of the ongoing service they could provide in tailoring systems to the particular needs of customers.

By 1980, however, the demand for personal computers had created a second and very different market for software. In programming for PCs, the emphasis shifted from individualized service to packaged programs that were inexpensive and varied. Word processors, spreadsheets, and small-scale systems for database management became the most important products. For the most part, the old guard of mainframe programming firms did not fare well in this new market. The biggest winners were all new companies—Microsoft, which prospered on the strength of a special affiliation with IBM's first personal computer; Lotus, which very nearly cornered the market for spreadsheets with a package called 1-2-3; and Ashton-Tate, which established a beachhead in database programming and never retreated. The industry was effectively divided into mainframe and microcomputer programming houses.

There are large and small participants in both spheres, but one of the distinctive features of the software industry is its fragmentation. The largest mainframe house, Computer Associates, generates annual sales of approximately $600 million. This figure represents less than two percent of the global software market, which currently totals about $30 billion. The biggest microcomputer programmer, Microsoft, has a slightly smaller slice of the pie. This state of affairs is in stark contrast to the computer-hardware industry, in which one company, IBM, controls nearly half of a $100-billion worldwide market. The upshot is that software companies tend to succeed either by doggedly laboring to please their customers or by being in the right place at the right time. No one company is large enough to overwhelm the competition with unmatchable investments in research and development—the kind that might substantially advance the state of the art in software.

A DEMANDING TRADE

In its most elementary form—in the creation of stand-alone programs to perform single, well-defined tasks—the work of software companies and their legions of programmers sounds deceptively simple. It involves three steps:

defin-
ing the prob-
lem, devising a plan to
solve it, and translating that solution into a language that computers can understand. Even for simple programs, however, the
process is rarely straightforward. Among other things, the programmer has to find solutions that accommodate the supremely me-
thodical way that computers operate.

An example of this orderly work style—and the demands that it places on creators of software—is seen in the way that computers are programmed to put lists of numbers in order. Such sorting, tedious for humans, is the kind of job that computers do particularly well. A classic software sorting routine is embodied in a program called Quicksort, written in the 1960s by the eminent British computer scientist, Tony Hoare.

Quicksort begins by instructing the hardware to choose a number near the middle of the list and form two groups—one for numbers larger than the selected one and another for those that are smaller. The program then puts one of the groups in order by repeatedly subdividing it in the same fashion, until it can be partitioned no more. When the second group has been given the same treatment, all the numbers are in sequence. Even the smallest of computers can do this kind of sorting very rapidly, but the software solution does not readily resemble the way a human would approach the same task. The programmer was forced to think in a different way.

Unfortunately, even simple programs often require several computer solutions as efficient as Hoare's, and a complex program may require them by the dozens or hundreds. Another formidable aspect of producing software is the need to make the expression of programming instructions nothing short of letter perfect. Such accuracy is necessary because the computer will interpret the code with absolute literalness. Even minor details, such as misplaced punctuation, mis-cited line numbers, or a lowercase *l* used in place of the numeral 1, are enough to make a program fail or bring the computer to a screeching halt.

These fundamental difficulties are merely the beginning for software producers. Nowadays, the creation of simple, independent programs is mainly a pursuit for hobbyists. Professional programmers spend the bulk of their time modifying and linking together software routines that already exist. As they have learned to create more complex programs, they have turned their attention to building and refining systems of software that are capable of performing many different jobs, and that grow or adapt to changing needs. For example, the computer system of an airline might book reservations, track the whereabouts of luggage and freight, orchestrate in-flight meals and movies, chart the maintenance and availability of aircraft, and perform literally dozens of additional functions. If the airline wants to personalize its service by giving ticket agents the ability to append notes to the flight plans of cus-

tomers, it calls in the programmers to extend the system further to include a capacity for writing and editing.

When software development reaches this level of complexity, it is referred to as systems programming, and it bears only a faint resemblance to the creation of stand-alone programs. The three basic steps—defining the problem, planning a solution, and expressing instructions to the computer—all grow exponentially more difficult because of the ways that programs tend to interact and disrupt one another when they are linked together *(pages 16-17).* Most software systems evolve over a period of years, with new capacities added as hardware advances make them practical. The many constituent programs may be revised for any number of reasons, some of which may have nothing to do with the quality or efficiency of the existing system. Examples are changes in tax laws, organizational restructuring, or shifts in a company's strategy. The revision process, whatever the motivation for the changes, is referred to as "maintenance" within the software industry.

It is not unusual for programmers assigned to overhaul the software system of a large institution, such as a telecommunications company, a manufacturing firm, or a nationwide automobile-rental agency, to be swamped by the diversity of the programs already in place and their interrelatedness. Chances are good that the maintenance crew will not fully understand the code that makes the existing system work. After all, that code may have been written years before by a team of programmers, and those programmers may or may not have left adequate written descriptions of their work. And the code may have been altered or refined many times by other teams in subsequent years. With each successive modification, complex programs tend to become a little more difficult to change.

The depth of the problems that characterize systems programming was first demonstrated by a combined hardware-and-software development effort conducted by IBM during the early 1960s. The eventual success of this project, which yielded the landmark System/360 computers and an innovative assortment of programs called an operating system, assured IBM's position as the dominant player in the computer industry for decades to come. At its inception, however, the project was a high-risk gamble with the potential to severely damage the company's fortunes. For a time, the outcome of the entire endeavor hinged on the ability of IBM software engineers to piece together a troublesome latticework of computer programs.

THE SEEDS OF SYSTEM/360

In the summer of 1961, IBM was selling computers at a robust clip. Its sales had grown at about 16 percent each year since 1955, and some of the company's current machines, such as the 1401 line of business computers, were big hits, promising to harvest profits well into the future. But in spite of the climb of corporate revenues toward the dizzying height of $2 billion per year, IBM Chief Executive Thomas J. Watson, Jr., and his trusted lieutenant, T. Vincent Learson, sensed an uncertain future for their products.

Like all other computers on the market at the time, IBM's machines were based on a transistor technology that seemed likely to become obsolete. The next generation of computers would almost certainly include integrated circuitry that could put dozens of transistors and other components on small chips of silicon. Computers built around these circuits would be dramatically faster and more powerful than their predecessors.

Adapting to that change would be a major challenge, but the company had mastered such transitions in the past. A deeper concern for Watson and Learson was that separate divisions within the corporation were selling completely unrelated families of machines, each with several members of varying power and price. IBM made computers for both scientific applications and business uses, and neither type of computer was very good at the other's job. The business computers could do only simple calculations efficiently, but they were absolutely accurate (so that banks, for example, would not have to round off fractions of cents). Business machines were also equipped to cope with large volumes of data, such as subscriber records for a popular magazine or population figures for a census. The scientific processors had a different set of mathematical tools. They were specifically designed to handle very large numbers, such as estimated quantities of atoms or stars, which might be expressed in powers of ten. And they could cope with an avalanche of repetitive calculations, which they executed less precisely than the business computers but much more quickly.

Because all of the machines, whether for business or science, had their own programming-language dialects, software written for one computer would generally not work on another. Watson and Learson knew that this general incompatibilty of software would gradually cut into the company's profits, because it made upgrading to newer or more powerful models a very expensive proposition. Customers who had already invested heavily in programming for one machine would be reluctant to repeat the expense, which could amount to 25 percent of the cost of the hardware.

The various IBM machines were also incompatible in the peripheral equipment they used. Each family of computers required its own uniquely designed input-output devices, such as magnetic tapes, disks, and punch-card readers. At any given time, fifteen or twenty different engineering groups were generating their own computer products, and each separate development effort had to be financed by the corporation. The company as a whole would profit if any portion of this research could be consolidated.

A COMPANY-WIDE CONSENSUS

To solve some of these problems, Learson sought to forge a consensus about what an ideal IBM product line would be. He set up a special committee composed of top representatives from all the company's fiefdoms. The panel was called SPREAD, for Systems Programming, Research, Engineering, and Development. For sixty days, the thirteen committee members lived and worked at a Connecticut motel not far from corporate headquarters, located at that time in New York City. They devoted long hours to brainstorming the issues and agreeing on a plan for the future.

Frederick Brooks, one of IBM's best computer-system designers, emerged as the dominant force in shaping the committee's recommendations. Then twenty-nine years old, Brooks was a North Carolinian who had earned a Ph.D. at Harvard under Howard Aiken—a scientist who in 1944 had collaborated with IBM in producing the world's first fully automatic computer. Looking back on SPREAD years later, the group's chairman, Bob Evans, called Brooks "brilliant, eloquent, and a natural leader."

The committee finished its deliberations three days after Christmas in 1961. On January 4, Brooks made a presentation of the committee report to a gathering of IBM's top executives. Today, that meeting and the SPREAD discussions leading to it are viewed as a watershed in business and computing history. Speaking for the committee, Brooks called not for a tempered introduction of new computers and gradual changes in the product line, but for a quantum leap in the evolution of computing. The SPREAD report suggested scrapping IBM's existing products—including the top-selling models—and abandoning the old ways of computer design for a bold, innovative approach that would be embodied in five new machines.

Perhaps the least radical proposal was one pertaining to the new integrated circuits. The SPREAD planners considered the experiments in microminiaturization just too risky at that point to be relied upon exclusively. Instead, they recommended the use of a hybrid transistor-and-chip technology. Many observers considered this stance conservative. But there was nothing conservative about another recommendation—to make all models in IBM's new line compatible members of a close-knit clan. Part and parcel of this idea was the unification of business and scientific computing: In the future, IBM customers who needed both capabilities would not have to invest in more than one expensive machine. In a corresponding move to unify software, the SPREAD committee proposed that IBM invent a universal high-level programming language that would be suitable for either business or scientific applications.

As Fred Brooks explained to the assembled executives, the key software-compatibility issue was whether or not programs could be made to run on machines of different sizes without first being rewritten. The SPREAD committee made this one of the goals for the proposed systems and went on to suggest that peripheral devices also be interchangeable. When it came to input and output devices, the New Product Line—as the project was called before it acquired a name—would attempt to give computer buyers the same flexibility that car buyers enjoyed with options and accessories. On the other hand, the committee felt strongly that the time had come for magnetic disks to replace tape as the preferred mode of data storage. They proposed that the disks be standard equipment and tape systems offered as an alternative.

DAUNTING CHALLENGES
The SPREAD report made no effort to conceal the many difficulties that the proposals implied—and the crux of the matter would be in the development of new software. The goals of the entire project hinged on the ability of IBM to create an operating system of unprecedented complexity. The operating system would

have numerous duties. It would direct the basic functions of the new computers, such as reading magnetic tapes and disks, displaying images on a monitor, or sending data to a printer. It would enable the hardware to understand and act upon applications programs, whether for producing charts and graphs, editing text, or manipulating numbers on an accountant's ledger. It would shuttle data and instructions among the various areas of the computer, such as the control unit, the logic unit, and main memory. And it would allow the computers to schedule a multitude of tasks internally without intervention by an operator so that the machines could work continuously at or near capacity. All in all, a prodigious set of responsibilities.

Nowadays, operating systems developed by or for computer manufacturers are more or less taken for granted. But prior to 1961, such flexible, general-purpose software was still a novel idea. Prospective owners taking delivery of a new hardware system counted themselves lucky if they received any software at all. Programming had to be started from scratch and required a detailed knowledge of the inner workings of the hardware. The operating system anticipated in the SPREAD report would make such learning unnecessary by providing a powerful set of standard commands that programmers could call upon to make use of the various hardware functions. In other words, the operating system would know everything about the hardware, so that programmers and computer users could get away with knowing very little.

The budget estimates for the operating system reflected the SPREAD committee's appreciation of the magnitude of the job. The programming costs were projected to be about $125 million—this at a time when the company's annual spending for all programming activities amounted to about $10 million.

THE CORPORATE GO-AHEAD

Unmistakably, Brooks and his colleagues were urging IBM to take a leap into the unknown. The changes that were being proposed could be roughly compared to General Motors scrapping its entire stable of well-known makes and models and introducing an all-new line of cars, covering the entire spectrum of customer demand, with an engine that ran on something other than gasoline. To accomplish the SPREAD recommendations required a development effort that would tie up practically all of IBM's resources for a period of several years. Failure would endanger the corporation.

Nonetheless, the decision of the men listening to the SPREAD report did not involve any great amount of soul-searching: "There were no real objections," Learson remembers, "so I said to them, 'All right, we'll do it.' " The formal corporate go-ahead—possibly the single most important business decision of the era—was granted in May 1962. On the advice of the marketing experts, the new computers were christened as System/360—a reference to their figurative ability to turn in any direction to face any type of problem. The operating system was given the acronym OS/360.

THE DIVISION OF LABOR

Learson appointed Bob Evans to oversee the development of System/360. Evans, in turn, gave Fred Brooks the job of establishing a basic architecture for all five of the new computers and of designing the three largest models, work that was to be undertaken at IBM's laboratory in Poughkeepsie, New York. Planning and programming of the operating system was also assigned to Poughkeepsie. Responsibility for the next smallest model was given to IBM's Hursley, England, laboratory, and the smallest one of the five computers, which was intended to be 100 times slower than the largest machine, was assigned to the lab in Endicott, New York.

Peripheral equipment and other system components were to be designed at several sites, while planning of the new programming language, PL/I (Programming Language One), was undertaken as a joint project with representatives of a consortium of IBM-computer users. They included Lockheed, Union Carbide, and Standard Oil of California.

One of the thorniest programming challenges was the goal of upward and downward compatibility, that is, making programs that would run on any model in System/360, regardless of which computer they were written for. Brooks and others wondered whether it would actually be possible to design programs for small machines that would not be grossly inefficient when run on larger, more powerful computers. But that problem paled before the prospect of trying to make software written for the largest machines run on the smaller models, which lacked the memory capacities of the giants.

At first glance, this task, which the SPREAD committee had proposed without any notion of how it could be accomplished, seemed impossible—like trying to design a single pair of shoes to fit everyone. Brooks set up a design competition among thirteen teams to find a hardware architecture that would overcome the memory disparities.

His strategy worked. The winning design stemmed from the invention of a device called a base register, which automatically abbreviates the memory addresses of programming instructions without permanently altering the instructions themselves.

Another elusive software objective to be resolved in a hardware solution was the need to salvage as many old programs as possible for use on the new machines. Brooks's engineers first ruled out the possibility of writing software that could automatically translate existing programs into the formats of System/360. They then developed a scheme that would enable the new machines to function, whenever necessary, like computers of the earlier generation by taking commands from preprogrammed read-only-memory (ROM) circuits that would be built into the System/360 computers. Learson staged a shoot-out to test the idea.

He pitted the System/360 Model 30 against its rough equal among the older generation, the Model 1401. Although the new computer took about 20 percent longer than the obsolescent one to complete the assigned tasks, Learson was delighted. With speed improvements expected from further refinement, the

A Bug at the Bank

Logic errors in a computer program, a common type of software bug, are usually not hard to fix. The difficulty lies in finding them. Stories abound of programmers toiling through the night before discovering the source of a problem.

Diagnosing logic bugs is a challenge for several reasons. The fault is usually subtle; otherwise it would have been caught as the software was designed or written. Like a balky engine that always purrs for the mechanic, bugs often appear only intermittently. Moreover, some logic bugs lurk perfectly camouflaged among the high-level-language instructions that make up most software, becoming visible only in the binary code—or its close relative, assembler code—that the computer actually uses to execute the program.

The routine for isolating a bug commonly begins with loading into the computer a type of program called a debugger. The debugger allows the programmer to see which instruction the computer is processing at any instant and where important values happen to be stored in memory, vital clues for solving the puzzle.

Debuggers can show no more than how software goes wrong. Figuring out why is up to the programmer. As explained here in the case of the erroneous bank balance, the solution is often simple, if obscure.

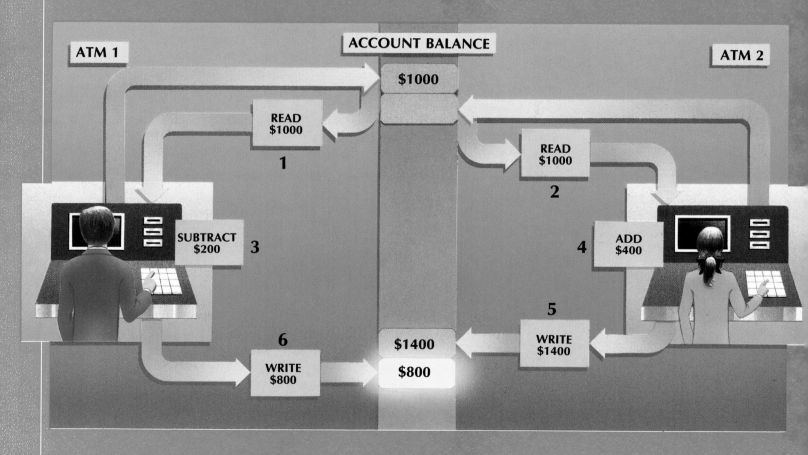

The bug revealed. A man withdraws $200 from an account held jointly with his wife (above, left). Almost simultaneously, at another machine, his spouse begins the deposit of $400. The husband's ATM reads the account balance of $1,000 from the memory at the bank's main computer (1), as does the wife's ATM an instant later (2). While the first ATM subtracts the withdrawal (3), the second ATM adds the deposit (4). Because withdrawals take slightly longer to process than deposits, the wife's ATM records a new balance of $1,400 before her husband's transaction is complete (5). His ATM, not knowing that the old balance has been increased, records a false one (6).

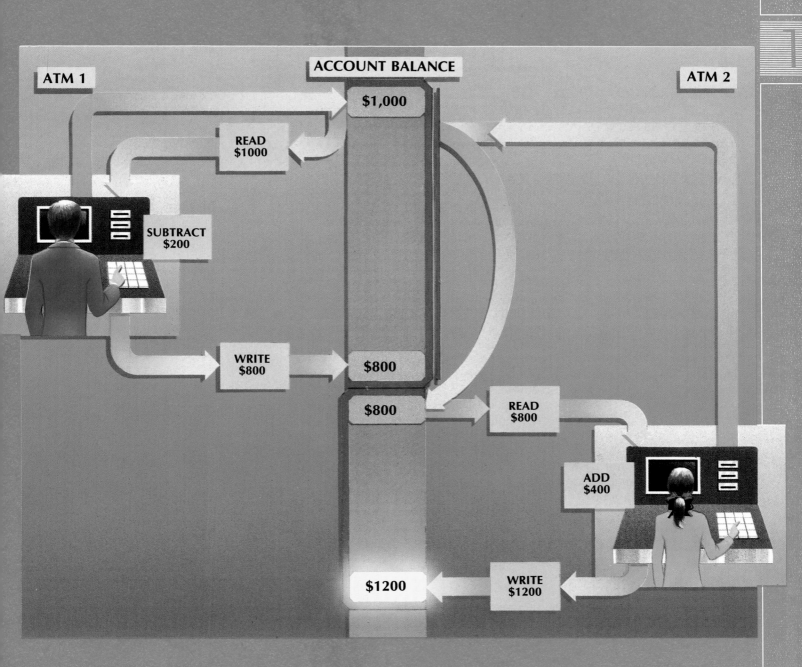

ATM 1

ACCOUNT BALANCE

ATM 2

$1,000

READ
$1000

SUBTRACT
$200

WRITE
$800

$800

$800

READ
$800

ADD
$400

$1200

WRITE
$1200

A simple fix. Barring ATMs from access to any account-balance memory location already in use solves the problem. With this arrangement, the wife must wait to complete her deposit until the computer has recorded her husband's transaction. At that time, her ATM is granted access to the account balance, which reflects the withdrawal. When the computer adds the wife's $400 deposit, the new balance is the correct one of $1,200.

Model 30 would easily outpace the Model 1401. Full development of the scheme for disguising the new as the old, a practice that came to be called computer emulation, began in earnest.

A SHROUD OF SECRECY

True to its reputation as a tight-lipped company, IBM revealed nothing about System/360 for fully two years. In the normal course of business, the company would eventually have announced each new model as it neared readiness. But Watson and other senior executives felt that the extraordinary revamping of the company's product line deserved special treatment, so they explored the possibility of announcing all five computers at once. The plan had the disadvantage of committing the company to a delivery timetable they were not yet certain they could meet. On the plus side of the ledger, such an arrangement would not only be dramatic business theater—and thus great publicity—but it might also encourage impatient customers to wait for the models that would be slowest to emerge from the development pipeline. And it would remove the temptation for eager IBM salesmen to leak word of models yet to come in hopes of dissuading potential customers from buying the competition's wares—tactics that were against company policy and raised legal questions.

On March 18, 1964, the company assembled thirty of its top brass at Yorktown Heights, New York, for a two-day final review of the project, including the pros and cons of simultaneously unveiling all five computers. This would be the last chance to derail the big event or to back out of any part of the whole risk-fraught venture without public embarrassment. The projections of the IBM sales executives were judged to outweigh the concerns about schedules. At the end of the second day, company president Al Williams stood and offered the group a final opportunity to voice dissent. Hearing none, he closed the meeting with an auctioneer's "Going, going, gone!"

On April 7, press conferences were held with much fanfare in sixty-two cities throughout the United States and in fourteen foreign countries. To the amazement of IBM's customers and competitors alike, plans for six new models (another large processor had been added to Poughkeepsie's project list during development) were made public.

A NOTE OF PANIC

Back in the development labs, however, some IBM programmers voiced concerns they had been keeping to themselves. As one executive said, "We were trying to schedule inventions, which is a dangerous thing to do." Moreover, evidence was mounting that the size of the programming job had been seriously underestimated. A sign of the problems that the software engineers were encountering was a string of requests from the programming team to increase the amount of memory in the new computers.

During the 1960s, IBM hardware systems still relied on a technology called core memory, which stored data on tiny magnetized rings suspended in a grid of current-carrying wires. Although the company was finding ways to manufacture such devices more cheaply, memory was still very expensive and was parceled out sparingly in even the most powerful computers. The software designers took pains to minimize the portions of OS/360 that had to be held in memory, opting whenever possible to have the operating system instruction brought in from magnetic-disk storage as needed. Nevertheless, they were finding that the instructions that had to be permanently resident were filling all the available memory, leaving no room for the applications programs that users would want to run. There was no choice but to increase the memory in the computers. As work on the operating system progressed and new problems were discovered, the basic memory allotment in System/360 rose from an original estimate of 8 kilobytes, or 8K (a kilobyte is 1,024 bytes), to 16K, 32K, and eventually 64K.

When it became clear that completing the operating-system code would be the crucial factor in shipping the new computers on schedule, Fred Brooks reassigned himself to devote full attention to the software problems, which now loomed disturbingly large. In the fall of 1964, Brooks further complicated his already-demanding schedule by beginning a long-planned withdrawal from his responsibilities at IBM in favor of a second career in academia. He began spending one week a month at the University of North Carolina in Chapel Hill, where he was establishing a department of computer sciences. To aid this transition, he elevated a trusted aide, Richard Case, to share his management duties. The two men occupied a single suite of offices and kept a joint calendar. IBM staffers with an appointment to see the boss never knew which boss it would be, but the arrangement worked.

Success on the job-sharing front, however, was not enough to ensure a satisfactory pace of progress. Software development on the scale of OS/360 was terra incognita, and as pioneers, the interchangeable managers made their share of mistakes, including one costly blunder that clearly underscored the perverse nature of large software projects.

While portions of OS/360 were still being designed, Brooks and two of his managers discussed the schedule and division of responsibilities for writing an important part of the operating system's specifications—that is, the detailed descriptions of what each component program should do, how big it should be, how fast it should run, and many other matters, such as how the various parts of the system should exchange data. The OS/360 architecture manager, who headed a small team charged with shaping the overall design of the operating system, said he had ten good people who could do the job in ten months—ninety days more than the timetable allowed. The manager for the control program, which would oversee the flow of work through a computer, countered that he could put 150 men to work at once and complete the job on time. He added that choosing his team would be a better use of manpower, since his programmers would otherwise sit idle while the architects completed the task. The architecture manager claimed that his colleague was mistaken, arguing that the control-program team was too large to be effective in a planning role and would probably run at least three months late anyway.

In the end, Brooks sided with the control-program manager. But he later had to admit that the architecture manager had been right on both counts: The specifications were finished behind schedule and caused more problems than they solved. By Brooks's reckoning, the flaws in this part of the operating system added about a year to debugging time in the later stages of the project and resulted in the waste of millions of dollars. The episode was just one among many in the execution of OS/360 that showed the flaw in the control-program manager's intuitive assumption that a large team of programmers could complete work more quickly than a small one. Such experiences led Fred Brooks to a maxim quoted by programming managers to this day: "Adding manpower to a late software project only makes it later."

OPENING COMMUNICATIONS CHANNELS

An important part of Brooks's and Case's strategy for keeping OS/360 on track was an emphasis on close communication among all parties to the effort. One of the most effective measures they took in this regard was the use of a project workbook—a carry-over from the company's tried-and-true approach to developing hardware systems. The workbook for OS/360 was a central repository for all of the technical information concerning the operating system. As changes were made in the specifications—many of them necessitated by changes in the hardware, which was on a parallel development path—they were scrupulously reflected in the book. Programmers had to keep abreast of modifications in their own sections of OS/360, and they had also to note revisions to other parts of the workbook, since it was possible, in theory, for a change almost anywhere in the intricate system to affect almost any other part. For example, a seemingly self-contained alteration in a section of code for verifying access to data files might cause an unexpected malfunction in a much more visible part of the system, such as the text editor.

Along with making the workbook a central feature of the creative process, Brooks and Case promoted a free flow of ideas by insisting on frequent informal meetings and telephone conversations. Even so, Brooks noted that the programming teams charged with implementing the designs of the OS/360 architects seemed inevitably to inch away from the plan. They would subtly alter the ways that the operating system accomplished certain jobs or diverge from specifications for the size and speed of their programs. Unannounced, such changes could be the source of problems in the overall workings of the system.

To counter this tendency, the two managers instituted a pair of more formal channels for keeping the project on track. One was a series of weekly half-day meetings, which brought together software architects, representives of the hardware and software implementation teams, and marketing officials, who were present to defend the interests of the IBM sales force. The assembly discussed new problems as they arose and outlined potential solutions to be studied. They also sought agreement on detailed solutions proposed for problems identified at previous meetings.

In addition, Brooks presided over annual two-week conferences. Attended by participants in the weekly meetings and also by the managers of their groups, these marathon affairs came to be known as supreme court sessions. Here, appeals were heard on large issues, such as the memory requirements of various parts of the system, and small ones, such as the nature of the typeface to appear in the user manuals—anything at all that had been subject to extended dispute. The primary purpose of the conferences was to make certain that everyone involved in producing OS/360 understood the pros and cons behind project decisions and accepted the group's resolutions as final. Brooks commented later that these sessions were very productive and should have been held not once a year, but twice.

The exhaustive measures to ensure communication between teams working on different parts of the system seemed to be the only way to minimize the number of problems. Thus, every change had to be considered from the standpoint of the entire system and made known to everyone involved in the programming. Yet despite the attempts to herd all the operating-system programmers in the same direction, the software teams almost invariably failed to meet their scheduled delivery dates. It became clear that in developing a system of this size and complexity, traditional guidelines for projecting schedules, budgets, or manpower needs could be thrown out the window.

In the hope that a fresh look at the problems might help solve them, another respected IBM manager, Watts Humphrey, was assigned to review the deteriorating situation. Arriving in mid-1965, he decided that the company had no choice but to swallow its pride and "decommit" thirty-one of the more elaborate operating-system features promised in the product announcement. Early the following year, Tom Watson told a meeting of IBM customers: "We are investing nearly as much in System/360 programming as we are in the entire development of System/360 hardware. A few months ago the bill for 1966 was going to be $40 million. I asked Vin Learson last night before I left what he thought it would be for 1966 and he said $50 million. Twenty-four hours later I met Watts Humphrey, who is in charge of programming production, in the hall here and said, 'Is this figure about right? Can I use it?' He said it's going to be $60 million. You can see that if I keep asking questions we won't pay a dividend this year."

SHIPPING THE SOFTWARE AS IS
Despite the problems, the first shipments of shiny new System/360 hardware took place generally on schedule between April 1965 and January 1966. But the software shipped with the new computers was battered and shrunken by the ordeal of its creation. The operating system lacked many promised functions, and those that were delivered did not always work well. To achieve even this disappointing level of performance had required enormous effort. At the peak of activity in 1965, more than 2,000 programmers were working on OS/360, nearly ten times the number originally thought necessary. From 1963 through 1966, a staggering 5,000 person-years went into the design, creation, and documentation of the operating system. OS/360 cost more than the Manhattan

Project, which produced the first atomic bomb, and may well have been the most expensive privately financed project ever.

But with all its faults, and despite its backbreaking expense, the operating system was an epic achievement. It helped make System/360 one of the most important developments in the history of the computing industry. The software's versatility, wide range of functions, and capacity for handling large amounts of data greatly impressed IBM's customers. Sales of System/360 far exceeded the company's hopes, and the gamble in staking so much of its corporate wealth on the project paid off handsomely: In the six years following the introduction of the new product line, IBM's annual gross income increased 230 percent, from $3.6 billion to $8.3 billion. System/360 lasted long beyond the life of preceding computer lines, and in the form of its direct derivatives is still going strong. As late as 1982, the descendents of the System/360 machines still accounted for more than half of IBM's income. In that same year, Bob Evans spoke proudly of the endeavor: "None of us dreamed that System/360 would last more than five or ten years. But it has endured and is clearly going to last well into the 1990s, and who knows after that?"

THE FIRST, PERHAPS, BUT NOT THE LAST

The IBM programmers who helped make this happy ending possible were not alone in the troubles they had overcome. During the early 1960s, virtually identical headaches plagued developers of other large-scale computer programs. Such was the case with the Multics system, written for computers manufactured by General Electric.

A joint effort by the Massachusetts Institute of Technology and Bell Laboratories, Multics was to be the first commercial operating system to offer a feature called time-sharing. It would apportion to dozens of users tiny increments of the central processing unit's attention, each increment no more than a few milliseconds in length. Properly done, time-sharing would produce the illusion that each of the users had exclusive access to the computer. However, such an operating system would have to be almost as elaborate in its own way as OS/360.

The roots of Multics (Multiplexed Information and Computing Service) can be traced to advances in hardware that made it possible to partition computer memory very finely and yet address it efficiently. This novel hardware configuration, called dynamic address relocation, allowed data in a computer to be used by more than one operator, and thus made time-sharing practicable. Researchers at M.I.T. wanted any new computers that they might purchase to include the feature and suggested to IBM that it be made a part of System/360. But the IBM development team had neither the time nor the resources to take on this additional challenge. As a result, M.I.T. bought a rival system from General Electric, which was modified to suit their purposes, and then joined-forces with Bell Labs to make time-sharing work. Fernando J. Corbató, a professor of electrical engineering at M.I.T., headed the development effort.

The group set lofty technical and performance goals. High among them was reliability. Computers running Multics should be able to operate unceasingly. No single component should be so critical that a breakdown or routine maintenance would knock the system off-line. Like System/360, Multics would be as adept at processing masses of accumulated data as it was to be speedy at crunching numbers. In addition, the system was planned to allow for the sharing of data and at the same time to protect confidential information completely, and it would have the potential to be extended and adapted to new demands. Almost from the start, however, the project was bedeviled by troubles.

UNEXPECTED PITFALLS

Like OS/360, the Multics team had greatly underestimated the difficulties that lay ahead. Corbató later admitted he had no idea so many things could go wrong. One source of difficulty was that there was virtually no software at all for the GE computer when the Multics programming began. Normally programmers begin with at least a small library of existing software, such as code that tells the computer how to display characters on a monitor or how to read input from magnetic tape. With no such programming to build on or use as tools, Multics was plagued by false steps, continually receding completion dates, and a need for special research projects.

For example, to improve efficiency, project leaders decided to provide their programmers with a high-level language, unusual for such projects in those days (most programming was done directly in the ones and zeros of machine code). Such languages allow programmers to frame their instructions to the computer in something approaching normal spoken English. The Multics programmers used PL/I, a product of OS/360 that attracted few supporters outside IBM. In the end, noted Corbató, the language contributed to the success of the project. It freed programmers from the minutiae of machine code, allowing them to spend more time analyzing their own work and looking for better ways to do things. At the start, however, the value of the decision was far from obvious. A high-level language is useless without a program called a compiler, which converts the English-like high-level statements into machine code. Compilers for PL/I were available, but they were for IBM central processing units, and the code they produced was gibberish to the General Electric CPU. Thus, an early imperative for the Multics project was the creation of a compiler, itself a complicated piece of software. Building it took several years, and until it was finished, no programming could actually be tested on the computer.

The software was built in modules, which are sections of programming devoted to particular functions, such as assigning memory locations or creating scratch files to hold data until it is saved. The work was broken up in this way so that different parts of the system could be fashioned at the same time. When the independently written modules were grouped together and tested, they did not perform at all as expected. Corbató concluded that the poor showing was mainly the result of a misbegotten attempt to make the system capable of too many things. He noted that the operating system was so big that individual programmers had no inkling of the effect that a particular module might have on the behavior of the whole. Overwhelmed designers found they could iron out flaws only by repeatedly trying fixes and testing them until they got the software right, a time-consuming process they had not planned for in the budget.

Programmers left, as they do on just about any long-term project. But the personnel turnover hurt much more than in ordinary business, because bringing new programmers up to speed on the system took six to nine months and diluted the efforts of other, more experienced team members. Ironically, a shortage of computer time—the very problem Multics was trying to solve—was also a hindrance in developing the new operating system. Without time-sharing, each programmer had to wait in line for the compiler. Corbató, like his counterparts at IBM, tried to speed things along by recruiting additional programmers, but the project fell further and further behind. Instead of lasting two or three years, it took five years to complete.

Despite delays, Multics was an eventual success. In the late 1970s the system was offered commercially by the Honeywell Corporation, which had purchased General Electric's mainframe computer business.

PROGRESS ON THE SOFTWARE FRONT
Multics and other time-sharing systems fulfilled their goal of providing ready, on-line access to computers, and in doing so, they considerably eased the difficulties of software production. The consequences of each statement in code was quickly made obvious. Time-sharing eliminated the slow turnaround time that had plagued programmers in the days of batch processing fat stacks of punched computer cards. It allowed interactive programming—the immediate computer response to programming ideas. Working directly at a terminal and carrying on a dialogue with the computer, a programmer was much more likely to understand the ramifications of programming decisions, because the consequences of each statement in code was quickly made obvious.

Nowadays, most programming is done on personal computers or on work stations linked to larger machines. Interactivity is a given. At the same time, high-level languages have greatly advanced since the days of PL/I. Hundreds of high-level languages have appeared since the early 1960s, and a dozen or so, including BASIC, Pascal, FORTH, and C, are in widespread use.

Despite the improvements, many problems remain, and the true capabilities and limits of programming are hotly disputed. No organization has a greater stake in these issues than the U.S. military establishment. One of the world's largest computer users, the Defense Department allocates billions of dollars every year to development and maintenance of software. Much of this money is spent on the programs that have become an integral part of weapons systems.

One project currently under development—the anti-ballistic-missile defense system, called the Strategic Defense Initiative (SDI), or Star Wars—will depend on a relatively new genre of software called distributed systems. Such software is used for labyrinthine networks of computers, currently used in tasks that range from trading in stocks and bonds to military data communications. Distributed systems entail a leap in complexity beyond even the most elaborate stand-alone system, and the network envisioned by the SDI planners figures to surpass them all. The debate among scientists about whether the proposed system is achievable has made the shortcomings and difficulties of software development a subject of much public speculation.

The core of SDI will be a computer system capable of identifying enemy missiles hidden in a swarm of decoys and then coordinating a large arsenal of weapons to destroy the incoming warheads. The system will depend on thousands of independent computers, sensors, and weapons-guidance controls located all around the world and in space. It will be expected to operate effectively even in the event that enemy countermeasures knock out portions of the system.

A leading critic of this ambitious effort is David L. Parnas, a professor in the Department of Computer Science at the University of Victoria in British Columbia. Parnas has spent more than twenty years in software development, much of that time devoted to military research. He is considered a leading theorist in computer science and has made substantive contributions to the improvement of programming methodologies. His involvement in the Star Wars question began with participation in the Panel on Computing in Support of Battle Management, convened by the Department of Defense. The panel was asked to identify the computer science problems that would have to be solved before an effective SDI shield could be deployed. On June 28, 1985, having concluded that the likelihood of successfully developing the SDI computer systems was minuscule, Parnas submitted his resignation, accompanied by a detailed explanation of his reasoning. He disavowed any political motivation in arriving at his conclusions, but based his skepticism on what he considers to be a clear-eyed critique of the current state of the art in computer programming.

The essential flaw in the SDI scheme, as far as Parnas is concerned, is that it ignores the fact that software is now and always has been a trial-and-error craft. In his words: ''The lay public, familiar with only a few incidents of software failure, may regard them as exceptions caused by inept programmers. Those of us who are software professionals know better: The most competent programmers in the world cannot avoid such problems.'' As surely as ants appear at picnics, bugs will appear in programs.

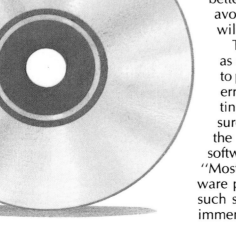

The people who produce computer code still spend at least as much time testing and correcting errors as they have devoted to producing the initial programs. Despite this recognition of the error-prone nature of their work, software companies rarely tinker with new programs to the point where the code is assuredly correct. Rather, they take their programs to market when the rate of discovery of errors slows down to a level that the software managers consider acceptable. As Parnas points out: ''Most products come with an express or implied warranty; software products often carry a specific disclaimer of warranty.'' But such standards are not good enough, in Parnas's opinion, for an immense real-time software system such as SDI, which must be reliable the first time it is used. The Star Wars software will presumably be used only once, if at all, so the break-in period that is routine in the creation of most software simply will not be available. The system can be tested only against computer simulations of reality. In Parnas's view, that will not be adequate.

THE ESSENCE OF SOFTWARE

The heart of the problem for programmers is the inherent complexity of computer software, which stands in stark contrast to the predictability of hardware technology. There is a fundamental difference between the two—a difference that will not necessarily disappear as the software technology improves. David Parnas sums up the problem this way: "Surprises and unreliability occur because the human mind is not able to fully comprehend the many conditions that can arise because of the interaction of (software) components." It becomes impossible for people to remember program logic when the importance of various kinds of data varies with the circumstances or when there are many decision points (each of which sends the program along one path if a certain condition occurs and an alternative path if it does not occur). In other words, programs tend to be filled with the software equivalent of the "ifs, ands, or buts." Just as in ordinary human language, these conditional elements produce statements that are convoluted and obscure. Unlike normal language, however, the conditionality cannot be eliminated simply by saying things more clearly. It is the very essence of the software.

Most computer scientists accept the fact that flaws will almost certainly occur in the first version of any program. But in spite of this somewhat fatalistic view, they generally agree that it is precisely through the process confronting "impossible" missions, such as OS/360, Multics, and Star Wars, that the field of computer programming gradually inches forward. In the words of Richard Case, who teamed with Fred Brooks on OS/360: "Computer hardware is the collection of things that we know how to do, and the software is everything else." Be that as it may, most people involved in computer programming are looking for ways to make their work just a little bit easier and more predictable, starting today.

Power Tools for Programmers

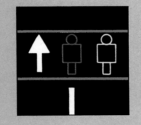

Of the bugs exposed during the testing of new software, the most difficult to fix are likely to come not from mistakes of programmers but from flaws in the design of the program. Getting the design right is the responsibility of systems analysts—software designers who translate the yearnings of computer users into plans for software that will satisfy them. But this is easier said than done. Useful programs are complex. Multiple threads of logic intersect so intricately that keeping track of them exceeds, for all practical purposes, the capacity of the human mind for such endeavors.

Fittingly, special programs can relieve systems analysts of this burden and permit them to focus their attention on the grand design of a software creation. These electronic helpers are known as tools for computer-aided software engineering, collectively dubbed CASE.

Such programs are typically classified either as front-end tools or back-end tools. Chief among the back-end variety are those that automatically translate a blueprint for a software system into a program that a computer can run. As explained on the following pages, the blueprint comes from front-end tools. The front-end programs impose an orderly approach on the process, help analysts probe the logic of their design, and allow designers to see how their software will function before a word of the program code is actually written.

CASE software is expensive; a complete toolbox can cost several thousand dollars per analyst. Even so, CASE can be a bargain. Producers of software that have taken full advantage of the assistance that CASE offers have reported productivity gains among their designers and programmers of up to 600 percent. Furthermore, CASE-designed software is easier to modify than programs produced without benefit of these digital tools. Improvements are regularly the source of new errors in computer software. CASE allows alterations in the design to be as thoroughly tested as the original before they are coded and disseminated.

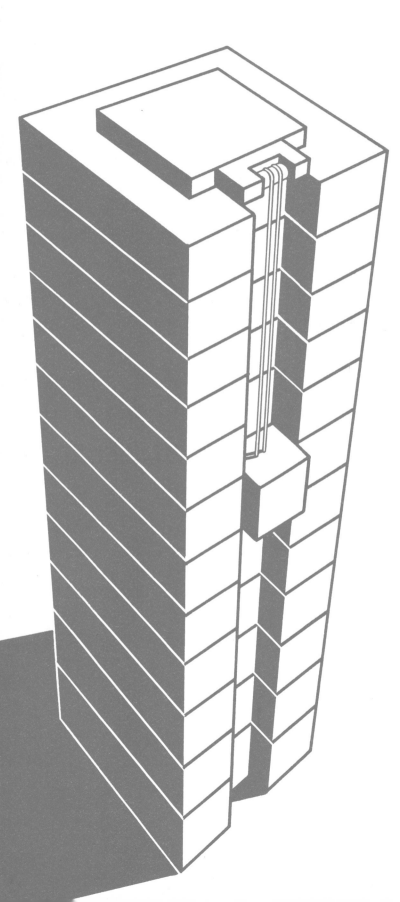

Components of a CASE System

CASE systems build a complex computer program as a hierarchy of component modules. Working downward from the top of the hierarchy, a systems analyst specifies in exhaustive detail the tasks that each module is to accomplish. The deeper into the structure the work advances, the more complex the proceedings become.

In the depths of the hierarchy, the modules of complicated programs become so intertwined that no human can keep track of them. Here the software-design process may falter. Increasing the number of analysts often compounds the problem; the advantage of splitting the program into smaller, more manageable pieces is offset by the burden of coordinating the designers' activities.

CASE takes over this responsibility, keeping track of all the details so that no inconsistencies arise to prevent the various parts of the program from working together as an integrated whole. In addition, a CASE system helps analysts to design a module for each program function, to establish hierarchical links between modules, and in order to determine whether the program will perform as intended, to test a design before coding begins.

As shown at right, a CASE system needs several components to perform these services. Though all are valuable, the foundation for the entire enterprise is a computer language specially tailored for designing software. Unlike programming languages, which customarily view computer software as a list of commands that tell the machine what to do, a CASE language sees a program as a complicated mechanism that can exist in many so-called states.

Almost any kind of program can be visualized as a state-based system. In a telephone network, for example, each section of wire must be in one of two states, busy or free. The state of the whole network at any instant consists of the states of the individual circuits. States, in turn, are governed by specific conditions or circumstances. A private line is in the busy state, for example, if any of the telephones connected to it is off the hook. Rules called transitions are also required. As the name suggests, transitions lay out the process for changing from one state to another.

On the following pages, the CASE method will be applied to the creation of control software for another familiar state-based system—an automatic elevator.

Describing the program. Function modules are the tasks that, taken together, embody the design of a software system. Each module has three components: inputs (keystrokes perhaps); input-dependent controls, or rules to follow (such as: Look up a keyboard signal in a table to find its meaning); and outputs that result from following the rules (the appropriate character appears on the screen).

Analysis aids. CASE systems use the contents of function modules to prepare documentation—lists of all the inputs, rules, and outputs for each module—and to display the same information in a type of table called a matrix. Documentation lets analysts unfamiliar with a project understand it quickly, while matrices flag missing inputs or outputs to help keep the program free of errors in logic.

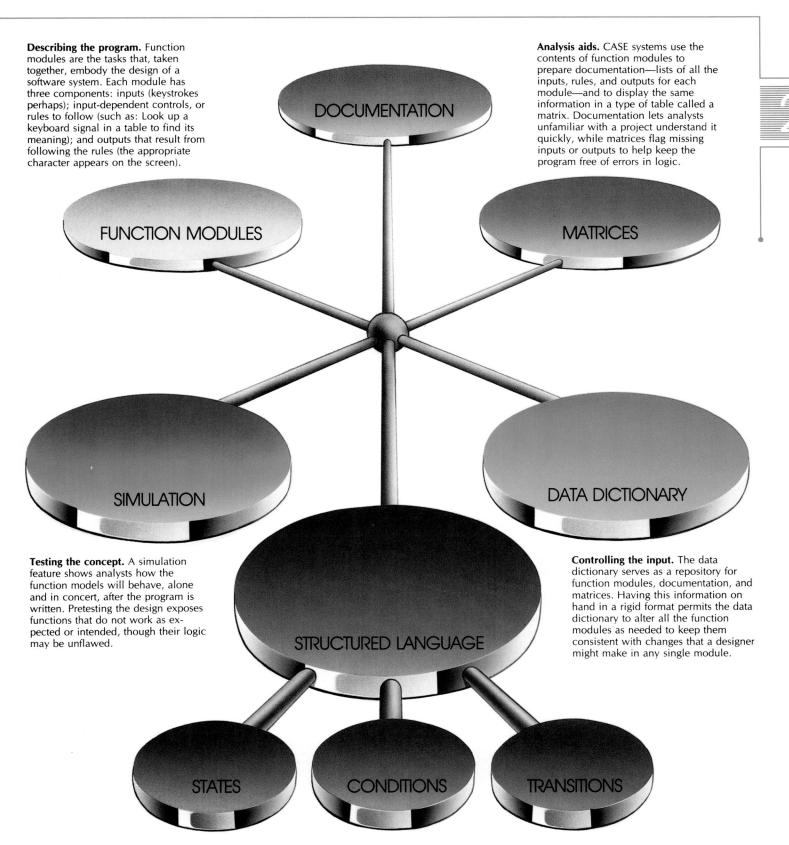

DOCUMENTATION

FUNCTION MODULES

MATRICES

SIMULATION

DATA DICTIONARY

STRUCTURED LANGUAGE

STATES

CONDITIONS

TRANSITIONS

Testing the concept. A simulation feature shows analysts how the function models will behave, alone and in concert, after the program is written. Pretesting the design exposes functions that do not work as expected or intended, though their logic may be unflawed.

Controlling the input. The data dictionary serves as a repository for function modules, documentation, and matrices. Having this information on hand in a rigid format permits the data dictionary to alter all the function modules as needed to keep them consistent with changes that a designer might make in any single module.

Speaking the language. For writing function modules, a CASE system includes a programming language tailored to the task of describing each function in terms of states, conditions, and transitions.

Focusing on Function in System Design

Function Modules

As input, the GO TO A FLOOR module *(below, center)* accepts the car's next stop from RECORD AND ARRANGE CALLS. Based on the car's current floor and direction of travel, which enter GO TO A FLOOR as controls, the module produces, as output, commands for operating the motor. Like GO TO A FLOOR, the other two modules also have appropriate inputs, outputs, and controls, all of which are recorded—along with the hierarchical relationships between the modules—in the data dictionary.

States of the Functions

Instructions (output) from GO TO A FLOOR to MOTOR CONTROL depend in part on whether the elevator car is in motion. The analyst records this distinction in the data dictionary as two states for the system— moving and stopped.

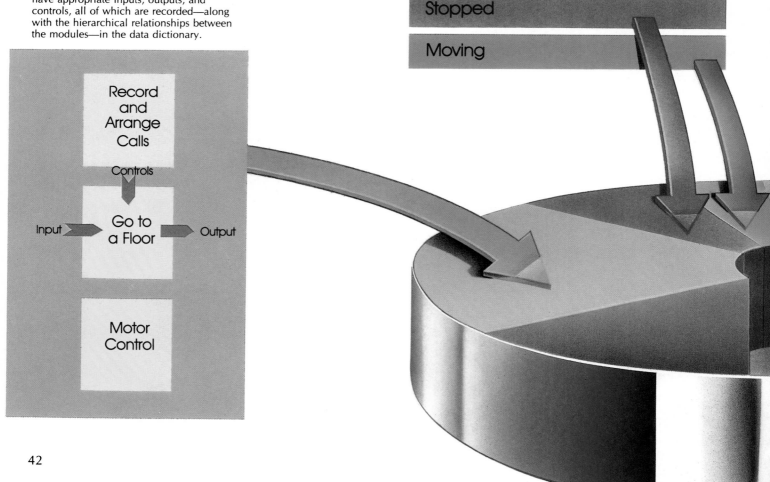

Record and Arrange Calls

Controls

Input Go to a Floor Output

Motor Control

Stopped

Moving

To a casual observer, an automatic elevator system seems complicated indeed. It must accept requests for service and assign a priority to each. The car must rise or descend, and it must stop at appropriate floors. Doors must open and close at the right moment and reverse direction when they are blocked. An idle car can be sent to a specific floor to wait for a call. Cars can be taken out of service or reserved temporarily to handle freight.

Hundreds of computer instructions are needed to make such a system work smoothly and efficiently. Yet analysis of the requirements for an automatic elevator reveals that the entire range of tasks can be accommodated by a program having a design so spare that it consists of just three function modules. One handles requests for service. A second keeps track of the car's current location and where it must stop in order to fill the next request for service. And a third function module controls motors that move the car.

The illustrations on these pages show how a software designer describes a simplified version of one module to a CASE system. In principle, the same process applies to the other functions. CASE, by requiring that all the modules be structured according to universal principles, helps assure that each function in the finished elevator-control program works faultlessly with the others.

Conditions for Each State

Commands to MOTOR CONTROL depend on the elevator car's location relative to its destination. For a stationary elevator, no command would be issued if the car was at the correct floor. If the elevator was moving, an order to stop the motor would depend on whether the car had reached its destination.

Stopped

Requested floor is the present location.

Requested floor is not the present location.

Moving

Sensor signal is the requested floor.

Sensor signal is not the requested floor.

Transitions between States

Commands to stop the motor and to start it, causing the car to rise or descend, are called transitions because they require changing from one state to another. (A rising car cannot descend without stopping.) Transitions are executed in accordance with the conditions established for both states. First the conditions applying to the current state are consulted to determine whether the state requires changing. If it does, conditions for the new state dictate the results of switching from one state to the other.

Transition from Stopped

If requested floor is present floor, stay in place; otherwise, go to a moving state. Then, if requested floor is lower than present floor, descend; otherwise, rise.

Transition from Moving

If sensor signal indicates requested floor, go to a stopped state.

Verifying Function Modules

A CASE system begins to reward designers after they have recorded all the details of a program's structure in the data dictionary. From this catalog, a CASE system can provide a variety of services that help keep a project on track and on time. For those in charge of the project, there are master management sheets. These charts show the status of each program module—who is working on it, whether it is finished, and its location in the data dictionary.

The system can also be asked to produce a description of the entire program or any of its parts, a feature that allows analysts working on one module of the program to see what

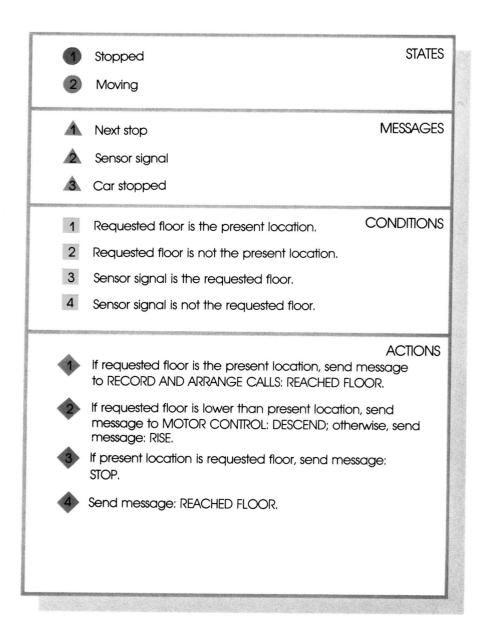

A LEGEND FOR A MATRIX

In the table at left appear the ingredients from which the CASE system constructs the matrix for GO TO A FLOOR *(right)*. States, inputs and controls, and conditions listed in the table come directly from the CASE data dictionary, as recorded there by the analyst. Actions are derived by the CASE system from outputs and transitions. Each statement in the list has a unique numbered symbol that permits the analyst to interpret the matrix.

to expect from modules that are the responsibility of other analysts. At some future date, when the software requires modification, this documentation makes it easier for a stranger to the project to understand its components, a necessary first step toward improving it.

But far more important than a CASE system's record-keeping prowess is its ability to link descriptions in the data dictionary of small parts of the project into depictions of larger parts—or even the entire program. State diagrams, for example, combine the states assigned to a module with conditions and transitions in a graphic representation of all the possi-

ble ways that a module can change from one state to another.

Even more helpful is a tool called a matrix (below), a table constructed automatically by the CASE system. A matrix presents all the components of a function module—states, inputs, outputs, controls, transitions, and conditions—in a form that makes it easy for a systems analyst to fathom the relationships between them, the better to pinpoint flaws in logic that will prevent the module from performing as intended. Errors are corrected by revising the contents of the data dictionary. For each matrix, the CASE system provides a legend (left) as an aid to interpretation.

An occupied cell. At the intersection of State 1 and Message 1, the car is stopped when it is notified of a call for service. If the request comes from the floor where the elevator is presently positioned, GO TO A FLOOR notifies MOTOR CONTROL that the car has reached the destination. If the next stop requested is a different floor, MOTOR CONTROL is instructed to raise or lower the car as necessary, and GO TO A FLOOR transitions from a stopped state to State 2, moving.

INSIDE A MODULE

This CASE-generated matrix for GO TO A FLOOR has a column for each of the module's two states and a row for each of its three inputs and controls, called messages. At the intersections of rows and columns, the CASE system displays conditions, actions, and states that pertain in the six possible combinations of states and messages. Three of the intersections, or cells, contain symbols; the other three are blank.

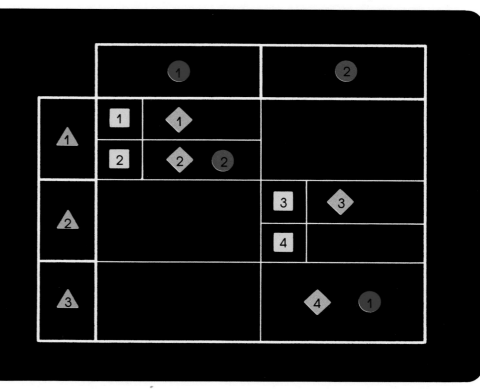

Empty cells. Vacant boxes in the column for State 1 are correctly blank; the messages alongside both boxes will not occur. In the case of the upper box, GO TO A FLOOR cannot receive a sensor signal with the car halted; the elevator must be moving to activate a sensor. Similarly for the lower box, the motor module would send a message confirming that the car has stopped only when changing from the moving to the stopped state, not while it stands idle. But the empty cell in the column for State 2 reveals a flaw in the software design; clearly, a car in motion must respond to a call for service.

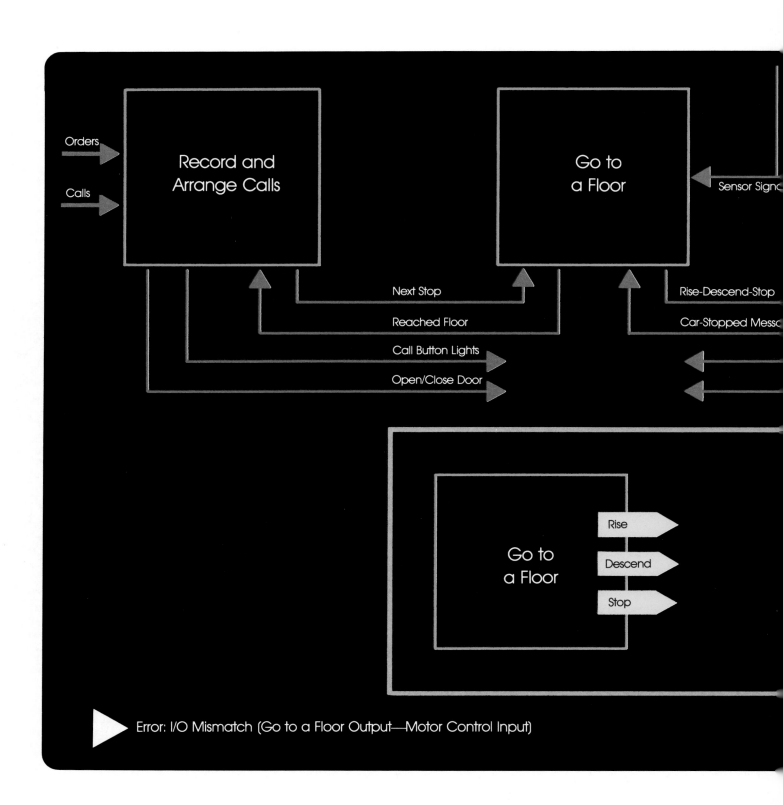

Orders

Calls

Record and
Arrange Calls

Go to
a Floor

Sensor Signa

Next Stop

Rise-Descend-Stop

Reached Floor

Car-Stopped Messc

Call Button Lights

Open/Close Door

Go to
a Floor

Rise

Descend

Stop

Error: I/O Mismatch (Go to a Floor Output—Motor Control Input)

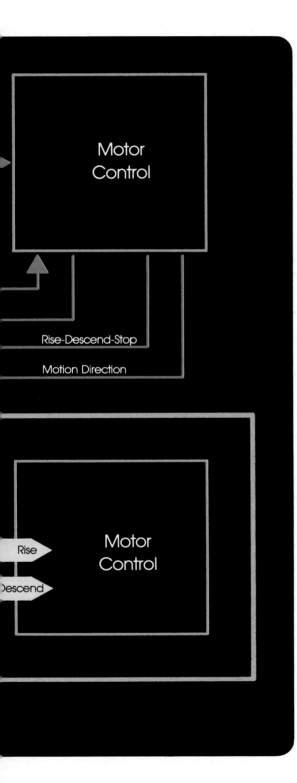

A Test of Integration

Perfectly designed modules offer no guarantee that the software will function when the parts are assembled. To step back from the trees for a look at the forest, an analyst can, in a few keystrokes, instruct CASE software to present a diagrammatic overview of the program design *(left)*.

Typically the picture is a simple one—the elevator system abstracted and stripped of minutiae. But as CASE retrieves information from the data dictionary to prepare the diagram, it rapidly and thoroughly examines the design in detail, searching out errors and inconsistencies similar to those already found—and corrected—within individual modules. To solve any such problem, an analyst recalls the module in question from the data dictionary, changes it as necessary, confirms new internal logic using a matrix, then asks CASE to reexamine the system as a whole. During this process, the software-engineering system automatically revises every facet of program documentation, assuring that everyone working on the project has the up-to-date information.

CASE also simplifies the task of revising software to satisfy a broad range of specific applications. For example, customizing an elevator program for a tall building or a short one requires nothing more than changing the maximum number of floors specified in RECORD AND ARRANGE CALLS. To create a multiple-elevator system, an analyst need do little more than clone GO TO A FLOOR and MOTOR CONTROL for each car and adjust the logic in RECORD AND ARRANGE CALLS that establishes priorities for answering requests for elevator service.

Ferreting out errors. In the top half of a computer screen, the CASE system displays the elevator-control program's three function modules. Arrows joining them are intermodule communications links that carry inputs, outputs, and controls. Other arrows represent signals from call buttons, floor sensors, and commands to the elevator machinery. A message at the bottom of the screen calls attention to an inconsistency between the outputs provided by one module and the inputs expected by another. Displayed in the lower half of the screen, I/O details reveal that the designer made no provision in MOTOR CONTROL for a "Stop" command from GO TO A FLOOR.

Simulation Testing Finalizes Design

In day-to-day operation, elevator systems must respond sensibly to a broad spectrum of conflicting signals. Someone wishing to descend might enter a car that is about to rise and push a button for a lower floor. Or a potential passenger rushing to catch an elevator can cause a closing door to reopen. In multiple-car systems, the work of fetching and delivering riders must be evenly distributed among all the elevators to assure prompt service while keeping the system's consumption of electricity to a minimum.

Systems analysts try to plan a program so that its logic can handle such circumstances in any combination, though this design explicitly addresses few, if any, of them. This approach

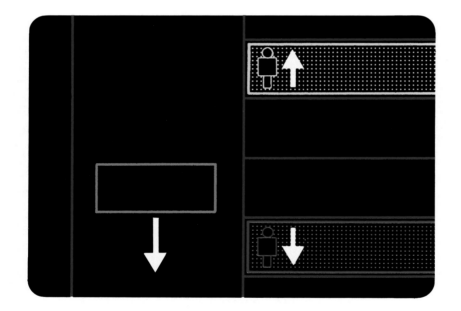

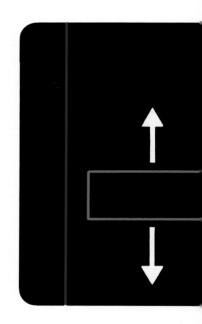

A simple case. In this simulation of the newly designed elevator-control software, the empty car receives two calls, one to go up from two floors above and one to go down from the floor below. In response, the elevator descends, following the rule that sends it to answer the nearest call first.

A case of paralyis. When the designer simulates a situation in which the car is called simultaneously from two equally distant floors, the system is unable to apply the nearest-floor rule and the car does not move. A solution might be to modify RECORD AND ARRANGE CALLS so that the elevator is biased to go one way or the other when two calls originate from the same distance.

usually yields a compact program that requires less computer memory and runs faster than programs in which every detail is spelled out. But such a design can conceal problems.

No matter how comprehensive such a design may be—and regardless of its having passed logical muster with a CASE system—it can fail to perform as desired. All too often, such shortcomings are not discovered until the finished software is tested. At this stage of development, repairs require not only redesigning the program but recoding it as well.

To help software engineers catch defects early, CASE uses the logic stored in the data dictionary to simulate the behavior of a system as it would respond to external influences. As shown on these pages for an elevator-control program, the computer displays an image of an elevator shaft in which a car rises and descends in response to passengers' requests.

Should the elevator perform unsatisfactorily, the designer returns to the data dictionary and alters the logic within the appropriate function modules, examines them once again as matrices and as a complete system, then subjects the program to the rigors of additional simulation. When satisfied that the logic is complete and correct, the analyst can release the design to programmers for coding, with a reasonable expectation that faults in the final product are the result of programming errors rather than design flaws.

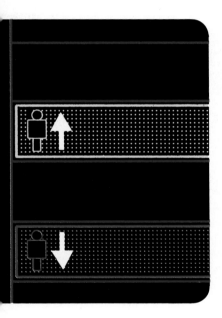

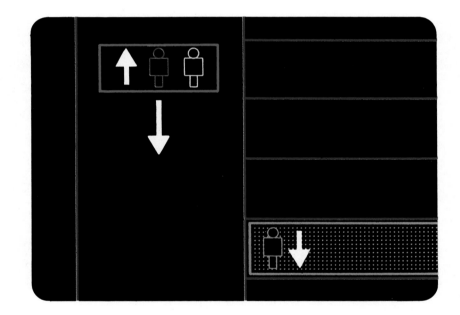

A direction command ignored. The elevator system is intended to honor commands issued by passengers already on board ahead of those issued from outside the car. But in this instance, the designer discovers that the riders' request to go up is overruled by a call from a lower floor. To rearrange the system's priorities, the software designer must return once again to RECORD AND ARRANGE CALLS and change the logic so that requests for service from outside the car are assigned a lower precedence.

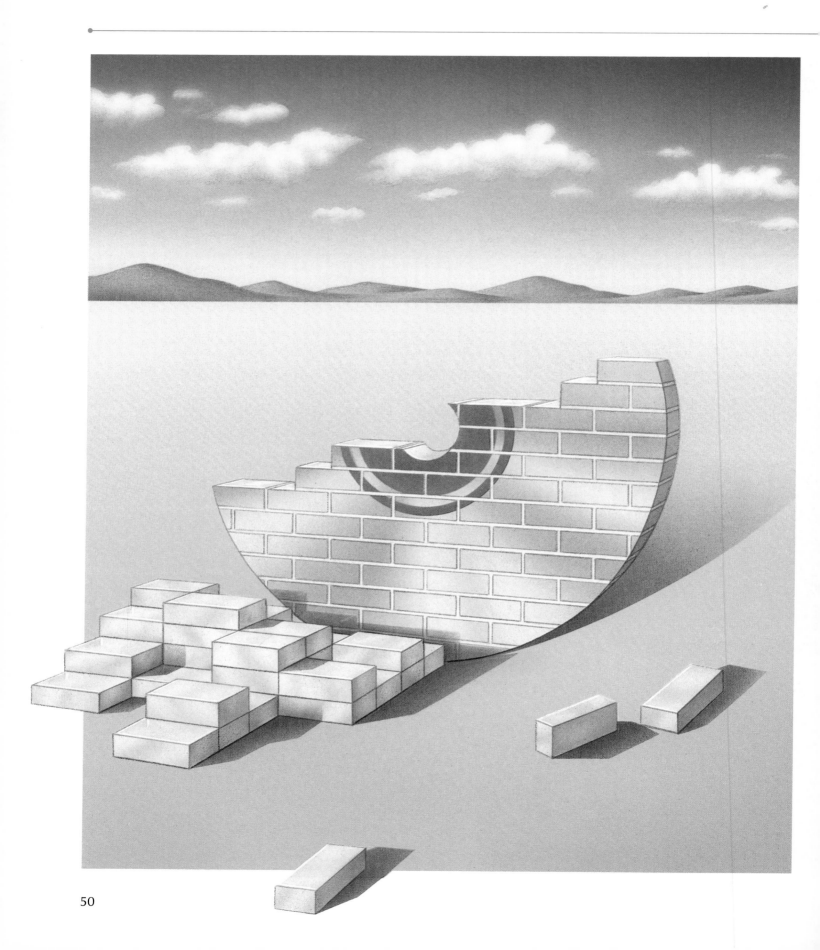

The Search for Efficiency

"We were in an abysmal state," said Herman Nichols, the purchasing manager for the East Bay Municipal Utilities District, or EBMUD. Among the largest publicly owned water companies in the western United States, East Bay Water pipes this essential fluid to more than a million California citizens who live in cities and counties east of San Francisco, but the utility's computer system had no software that could tell Nichols how much in the way of supplies and equipment were on hand.

Nichols was responsible for a million-dollar, 2,600-item inventory of pipes, valves, fittings, meters, and other essential material and equipment. The utility's financial computers reported on his inventory once a month, but no software was available to track day-to-day changes in warehouse contents. Determined to stock enough of everything to keep the water flowing, Nichols always erred on the side of buying more than he thought would be needed, an expensive practice that tied up huge sums of the utility's cash.

The data-processing staff at EBMUD's computing center told Nichols that they could write a set of programs for him. The software, however, would be batch oriented and therefore totally inadequate; it could at best provide periodic updates and reports on the status of Nichols's department. Even if such a system had been satisfactory, Nichols would have to wait more than a year before work could begin on his project, and it would have cost a fortune. The computer center estimated that writing the software would consume seven programmer years. Unable to justify such an expense, in 1986 Nichols signed up computer consultant Ross Mitchell of Newton, Massachusetts, to do the work. Mitchell finished the job in just fifteen months for about one-fifth the cost quoted by East Bay Water's own programmers.

To work this seeming magic, Nichols applied a novel approach to software development called computer-aided software engineering, or CASE. Owing much to developments in computer-assisted design and engineering software written for other fields, CASE is changing the way in which systems analysts and programmers approach the problem of producing complex software. Traditionally, project managers in the programming world have focused efforts to produce working software as quickly as possible on the so-called back end of the process—the actual coding, or writing, of the software. By optimizing that stage of software development, they hoped to reduce the cost of programming, do it faster, and improve on its quality enough to at least keep even with—and perhaps reduce—the software backlog, that vast number of systems, like Herman Nichols's, waiting in line to be written.

Productivity seemed to increase—but so did the backlog. The faster and more efficiently programmers worked, it seemed, the more their internal clients demanded of them in the way of software features and complexity. By the mid-1970s, the visible queue of software awaiting development in some organizations stretched four to seven years into the future. An invisible backlog—wish lists of projects not asked for—often held another two or three years' work. The high demand for software services that were in short supply led to higher and higher costs, and a chilling graph appeared from time to time in many a computer publication. It showed the cost of hardware far exceeding the cost of software in the early years of the computer age. But as time passed—and the hardware cost-line slanted satisfyingly downward—the software cost-line inclined inexorably upward. The clear implication was that declining computer prices would ultimately be offset by increasing prices for software.

This dismal forecast led some information-services (IS) managers (those in charge of chipping away at the software backlog) to turn, in the search for greater productivity, from the back end of the software-development cycle to the front end—the initial stages of programming in which the goals of the software are first set forth. Rather than asking how programmers might be induced to write more lines of code, these pioneers began to inquire how the design of a software system might be more accurately expressed to the code writers, hoping that precision in the earliest states of the cycle would lead to more lines of code per programmer-hour.

MEASURING PERFORMANCE

Lines of code is the best known and most widely applied measure of programmer productivity—and a logical one. More formally known as delivered source instructions, or DSI, this tally of output simply divides the number of lines in a program by the number of programmer-hours required to produce them. The rate is so dismally low—on the order of two lines per hour—because first drafts don't count. Only debugged, error-free code qualifies, and since debugging traditionally occupies as much as half a programmer's time, it is little wonder that complex, custom-written software systems carry price tags that make the wealthiest corporations and even the U.S. government blanch at the bill.

DSI can trace its roots to the 1950s, when programmers wrote computer code as strings of ones and zeros. Writing longhand on a coding pad having eighty spaces per line that corresponded to the eighty columns on an IBM punch card, code writers penciled in one central-processor instruction per line for transfer to punch cards. Finding the number of source instructions was as simple as counting lines of a program.

Computer time in those days was expensive. One software expert recalls that on his first day as a programmer, "my supervisor marched me up to this big computer, and said, 'There's one thing I want you to remember. We're paying this thing $600 an hour and we're paying you $2 an hour, and I want you to act accordingly.' " This kind of thinking led programmers to seek economies wherever possible. For example, to reduce the number of cards required to contain a program—and thereby minimize the computer time spent reading the program into memory—they soon began to write two or three instructions on each line, separating them with colons and semicolons.

Though efficient, this practice upset the DSI applecart. A simple count of lines in a program was no longer an accurate guide to the number of instructions being sent to the computer. Assembler languages, a step away from ones and zeros, increased programmer productivity because they represented long, multiple-instruction commands as one-, two-, and three-letter codes, easier to remember and to write without error than equivalent strings of ones and zeros. But this advance further confused the issue. High-level languages (FORTRAN was the first one widely available) went a step further, representing long sequences of assembler instructions in a single line of a program.

As computer languages advanced, it became impractical to count the number of processor instructions implied by each line of a program, so DSI came to mean "delivered lines of code." But with no way of knowing how many instructions each line contained, DSI lost much of its utility. For example, no direct comparison of productivity was possible between programmers working in different languages, because no two of them were equal in the number of processor instructions that they packed into a single line of code. Even within a language, some lines might contain more machine instructions than others, complicating productivity comparisons among programmers.

Inasmuch as software systems are not equally complex, a simple measurement like DSI can be misleading. One group working on a relatively simple set of programs might exhibit high productivity, while others equally competent—but working on a more difficult project—might appear to be relative dunces.

The Halstead metric, developed in the early 1970s by Maurice Halstead of Purdue University, attempts to solve this problem by handicapping software according to complexity. Halstead's method classifies every word in the high-level-language version of a program as either an operator or an operand. Operators are the actions that the software instructs the computer to perform—adding a pair of numbers, for example. Operands are the objects of these actions—in this case, the two numbers to be summed. Based on counts of operators and operands and the total number of times each appeared in programs he studied, Halstead developed formulas that yielded a score for computer code indicating its complexity.

Neither DSI nor the Halstead metric, however, addresses an important aspect of productivity: the difficulty of predicting how much work a program will require. Misjudgment on this front lowers the morale of a software development staff that is given too much to do within an unrealistically short time. It also has a disturbing effect on clients who, when a program falls behind schedule, almost invariably begin to question the competence of the people who are involved with the work.

In an effort to help software developers estimate more accurately the resources required to produce a piece of software, Allan J. Albrecht of IBM invented function-point analysis in the late 1970s. Instead of examining the completed code, function-point analysis probes the design specifications. In Albrecht's approach, a function point is defined as any input to the program, any output that it produces, any inquiry it is programmed to answer, any file of data that the software must consult, and each use of another program or subroutine. The totals of the different types of function points are weighted according to the difficulty of programming them. Outputs, for example, tend to be harder to accommodate in programs than inquiries. Function-point analysis produces a number that can be used to compare projects according to complexity. If one system has twice as many function points as another, it will also take about twice as long to develop.

Though seemingly a useful tool for software developers, functional analysis

depends on the presence of a complete and accurate program design, something that is all too often lacking. Furthermore, the task of actually producing such an analysis is burdensome. Some professionals in the software field, says Jim Webber, president of Omicron, an association of senior IS managers from major corporations, argue that this method "is so paper-laden that the overhead cost of administering a full-blown function-point measurement is too high."

William Garrett, chief of information services at AT&T, contends that "the area of measurement is the single biggest failure of IS." Having no reliable yardstick handicaps developers of software in their efforts to improve productivity: They cannot tell whether they are doing better or worse. For this reason, many of them have turned to a seat-of-the-pants approach: If writing a program under one set of circumstances consumes fewer resources than writing a similar program under other circumstances, then productivity is thought to have improved. A more objective reading results from assigning two independent groups of programmers to write identical software under differing conditions. The reasonable assumption is that any variance in productivity between the teams can be ascribed to the contrasting settings. This approach is so costly, however, that it is almost never used outside the rare defense project or a university setting where a computer-science professor might set two groups of student programmers to work producing two versions of the same software using different approaches.

MANAGEMENT ISSUES AND SOLUTIONS

Providing creature comforts and the right tools for the job can lead to substantial improvements in productivity. Experience has shown that the simple expedient of providing programmers with private offices can boost output by 10 percent or so. Spending more money on equipment also helps. The typical investment per programmer in the traditional tools of the trade—access to a terminal or a computer, word-processing software and a compiler for converting programs from a high-level language to machine code, a desk and a chair—averages three thousand dollars or so, not much more than the amount spent to equip general office workers. Yet some organizations have found that spending as little as ten thousand dollars per programmer for a higher-speed computer, a network to link them together, and office furniture designed to reduce fatigue can yield significant dividends.

The experience of TRW, a major supplier of software to the United States government and armed forces, illustrates the point. In a typical software shop at TRW, a programmer's workspace was once a spartan affair. Three or four programmers shared a rather small office filled with computer terminals, steel desks, filing cabinets, chairs, and bookcases. In some parts of the company, programmers were assigned to large open rooms known as bull pens. Although each person had a desk, the group often shared hardware that was located in another room. In a 1981 experiment that TRW called the Software Productivity System (SPS), programmers were given individual offices with wall-to-wall carpeting, soundproofing, and comfort-engineered ergonomic furniture. More powerful terminals offered much shorter compiling times and, connected to central mainframes, also facilitated the exchange of ideas between members of a programming team.

Some workers were less than pleased with the change. "I didn't feel like part of the team anymore," commented one individual. But he soon came to appreciate the advantages of his new work environment. "I'd close the door and grind away at my work, and the next thing I knew I was getting hungry. I realized it was 6:00 p.m., and I'd worked right through the day." For programmers involved in the SPS experiment, productivity soared 39 percent in the first year. "The results," recalled one TRW vice president, "were so good we were reluctant to believe them."

A STRUGGLE TO STAY EVEN

Such gains, though real, disappeared like water into a desert, in part through programmers' leaving work on time rather than working unpaid overtime late into the evening, and in part by demands for increasingly complicated software to streamline all manner of business activities. The more complex a system becomes, the longer each line takes to write and debug. The reason is simple enough. Each additional instruction that a software system is asked to accommodate, every extra decision that the programs' internal logic is asked to make offers rapidly increasing opportunities for conflicts within the software. Debugging time escalates, and hourly DSI declines. The best equipment and project-management techniques were not enough to make a substantial dent in the software backlog. A new idea was needed—and soon.

Programmers around the world write some fifteen billion lines of code each year; approximately 100 billion lines have been written in the three decades since 1955. But much of that programming is wasteful duplication of virtually identical features, reprogrammed anew for each internal client. In banking and insurance applications, for example, 75 percent of all new code executes common functions that appear again and again in different applications, in different languages, for different kinds of computers. One analyst has found that, of all new code written for business, less than 15 percent is unique or novel.

The problem seemed to suggest its own solution—collections of reusable software modules that can be copied and assembled into new programs. Of course, any software that is duplicated in large quantities for sale to computer users—from operating systems that run the machines to database programs and word-processing packages for personal computers—is reusable software. Software modules, however, are incomplete in themselves. They are software components that link together much as hardware parts such as microprocessors, disk drives, and printers can be assembled into a computer system. There are many such collections, large and small. Universities are hotbeds of this activity, especially in science and engineering departments where researchers commonly have easy access to programs written by their colleagues. Most others have been built by companies for their own use.

Even a modest effort in the direction of a software library can achieve worthwhile economies in business programming. In 1981, the Hartford Insurance Group in Connecticut began such a program. After seven years, their library consisted of thirty-five program modules, written in COBOL and tailored to the group's computer operations. Each of the fifteen complete programs and twenty subroutines—smaller programs intended for assembly into large ones—is fully documented and thoroughly reliable, having passed the rigors of actual use in the insurance business. Each of the insurance company's fourteen programming shops is encouraged to use the library and is required to disclose each month how useful the library has been to them. The reports reveal that as much as 40 percent of the code in new programs comes from the software collection, a figure that translates into a savings in staff time of about 225 programmer-days a month—or more than $600,000 a year.

Thoughtful management is an essential ingredient of such success. At the Hartford Insurance Group, for example, each programmer who submits code for the library receives a distinctive coffee mug to reward and commemorate participation. The best offering of the month brings the author a $300 reward. Steve Sposato, who administered the software library at Pacific Bell, tells of quotas established there encouraging programmers to either use the library or add to it; at Pacific Bell, says Sposato, "you're either a consumer or a contributor."

A software library must also have the equivalent of a comprehensive card catalog. To that end, Sposato devised a hierarchical index—a display of the library's constituent programs by type or category. With each programmer's work station connected to the library by network, withdrawing a program was as simple as moving a cursor down the hierarchy (it resembled a business organization chart) to the desired program and pressing a key. This point-and-shoot approach brought the module to the programmer's work station. A library must also be seen as valuable. Sposato delayed opening the collection to his public until it had been well stocked with programs. "If people log on to a library with little or no inventory," he explains, "they'll think it's a waste of time. When the library eventually accumulates a decent collection, you'll then be faced with trying to convince those people to log on again."

A handful of companies sell their collections to other software developers. The Raytheon Corporation, for example, has developed a full spectrum of business functions, commercially available under the name ReadyCode, that can be woven together with new code in an integrated system. With ReadyCode, up to 60 percent of the software for common business applications can consist of reusable modules, resulting in a 10-percent saving in the design of a new software system and a 60-percent reduction in the costs of programming and of adding new features to the software after it is complete.

REASSESSING THE SITUATION
Libraries of reusable software, the attentiveness of developers to the needs of their programming staffs, and even flawed measures of software productivity share a bias that the source of more reliable software at lower cost is to be found in the

code-writing process. If the complicated job of actually writing a program could somehow be simplified or made less labor-intensive, the software cost-line on the graph might at least begin to level off. But because this strategy has not lived up to expectations, another has come to the fore. Rather than focusing on the back end of the software-development cycle—programming, debugging, and maintenance—proponents of this new approach contend that the solution to the software backlog lies in the design stage of creating new programs. If the specifications for a software system could be complete and unambiguous at the outset, goes the argument, then code writing would become a trivial matter that could be automated, left to a computer.

Two items are crucial to achieving the goal. The first is a translator program, which would receive a description of the tasks that the new software must accomplish and translate the description into an intermediate language better understood by the computer. This translation would become the input to the second component, a software compiler—a program that produces the new code that will carry out the specified jobs. In automatic programming at its purest, a software engineer would write a formal statement in a high-level language—ideally in English—specifying the software's purposes in detail. From the back end would emerge bug-free code that would cause the computer to perform as intended.

That the back-end element of the formula has practical solutions has been evident since the 1950s, when the first FORTRAN compilers demonstrated that they could convert the language's high-level statements (many of which looked a lot like the mathematical formulas that engineers and scientists had always written on paper) into the ones and zeros of machine code. Since then, other compilers, written for many more recent languages, have advanced the art. However, the front-end element of the formula has been lacking. Not only is it difficult to translate English, replete with ambiguity and redundancy, into terms a computer can handle, but the demand for such a tool was for many years insufficient to impel the invention of one.

Interest was slight because of the nature of programming, of the people who practice it, and of software-development managers, who are themselves former programmers elevated into positions of authority. For every doting father who begins assembling a swing set in the backyard before reading every word of the instructions, there is a programmer who would rush into writing code before fully understanding a new system's objectives and how they are to be accomplished.

"The analysis phase," says Jim Webber, "requires interaction with the user, and that's not a role that a lot of information systems professionals are comfortable with." To do the job well, a systems analyst prowls a client's corridors conducting extensive interviews, asking hundreds of questions intended to reveal exactly how the organization operates in areas such as payroll or personnel records that it wishes to automate. Other queries expose tasks, impractical to perform manually, that the company hopes to accomplish with its new software system. Even if an analyst works earnestly, the client may not cooperate. "People don't want to sit around and talk about what they're doing," observes Webber, "they want to get right to it."

As recently as the early 1970s, when analysis of this kind was attempted, the results were often disappointing—even if all the parties involved appreciated

A Plague
of Viruses

Shortly before Christmas of 1987, a West German hacker slipped into a frequently copied program a few lines of extraneous code that made computer screens flash a holiday greeting. A warm pleasantry? Not really, for the code also read the address-book file in each computer it reached, then sent a duplicate of itself to those addresses as they were called repeating the process over and over. One recipient of this bad joke had access to IBM's corporate communications network Within two hours, some half-million Christmas greetings clogged the IBM network, shutting it down.

A much more sinister "computer virus" spread through hundreds of computers connected to the Hebrew University of Jerusalem. The virus was designed to destroy all data in each computer it reached, acting everywhere on May 13, 1988—a Friday. Fortunately, a programming error gave away its existence, and it was mostly eradicated before any harm was done. But at a bank in Tel Aviv, at a newspaper in Haifa, as well as at the university in Jerusalem, computers crashed on that date.

Such electronic vandalism is called a virus because it acts like a biological virus. It is small, often only a few lines of data It usually travels on a carrier—an ordinary, useful program It reproduces itself rapidly and easily, so that it can spread from host to host widely and wildly. On infecting a host it frequently lodges in a vital organ: the hard-disk permanent

A virus *(red glow)* enters the computer through an infected floppy disk *(above),* spreading into the RAM temporary *(yellow)* and hard-disk permanent *(silver)* memories. Below, a clean floppy and backup storage tape become infected from the RAM, while the hard disk infects other computers via telephone.

emory, from which the virus can emerge to infect other ograms and other computers. And it causes some unwanted ent to occur—perhaps nothing more wicked than the wish universal peace that once popped up in a commercial aphics program—but in most cases it is a malevolent attempt by a terrorist or a disgruntled employee to disrupt computer operations.

To explain how a computer virus works, Fred Cohen of the University of Cincinnati uses the analogy of a group of secretaries who work strictly by rote. "When the boss says do something, they look up that something in card files they keep. And when they find the appropriate notecard, they do whatever it tells them to do. If one secretary doesn't find the relevant card in his file, he goes to another secretary who does and uses that card. Imagine, then, the following sentence appears on one card: 'In your own words, copy this sentence onto all your other notecards, and if the date is after January 1, 1993, burn everything in sight.' That's how I teach people what computer viruses are."

Cohen was one of the first scholars to investigate computer viruses, which can be traced back at least to the mid-1960s, when what seemed to be a game tied up an early Honeywell mainframe computer. The game, named Animal, asked the user to think of an animal. If the program could not guess the user's choice from his keyboarded responses to questions, it asked the user to supply additional questions that would enable it to win the game. As it added to itself more and more questions provided by users, copying itself from work station to work station, the program grew until it almost overwhelmed the mainframe memory.

The viruses are not omnipotent. A virus that is written for a personal computer may not be able to function on a mainframe because the computers have different operating systems—software that serves as an internal traffic cop. Moreover, viruses can be cured with programs that mimic, then wipe out the infection. And protective software can ward off many viruses.

One antiviral program, called Canary, prevents network contamination by acting as bait. It is loaded onto a clean and isolated PC together with a new program that might be infected. As the computer code runs, Canary monitors itself for viral effects and reports any to the user. Another program, ComNETco's Virusafe, sounds the alarm if it notices unusual commands being sent from one program to another through the computer's operating system.

No practical measure, however, offers a foolproof defense against computer viruses. "The only way to protect everybody against them," says one computer security specialist, "is do something much worse than the viruses: Stop talking to one another with computers."

Contamination in RAM is erased once the computer is turned off, but it remains in the hard disk *(left)*. Once the computer is turned on again *(right)*, the virus becomes contagious and can spread from RAM once more.

the importance of doing a good job. The problem was that programmers and analysts had no way to be certain that they had asked all the necessary questions. A disorganized approach to the task left crucial information undiscovered. Resulting flaws in the software often remained hidden until the project was well along toward completion or undergoing tests by the user. By that time, the costs of fixing the problem were about the same as if the new approach had never been attempted.

A FRUSTRATING RAT RACE

In the opinion of Edward Yourdon, a young freelance computer consultant in the early 1970s, this state of affairs clearly could not persist if software development was to improve. Yourdon described the plight of the typical software project manager thus: "Your programmers generally quit after a year in your organization, and they always wait until the final stages of the project. And the documentation that you finally forced them to write turns out to be unreadable and completely inaccurate—or so you're told by the new programmer, who promptly throws the old coding and the old documentation into the wastebasket and begins anew. And on and on. . . ."

Acknowledged by his peers in the software business as a fountain of creativity, Yourdon began a crusade for a new approach to the initial stages that he called structured analysis. The name recalled earlier attempts to bring order to the chaos of the software-development process. Structured programming, for example, was an idea first expressed by the eminent computer scientist Edsger W. Dijkstra in a series of articles in the mid-1960s. His hope was to bring a hierarchical order to computer code, which traditionally blazed a meandering trail for its logic that was virtually impossible for anyone but the original programmer to follow. Shortly thereafter followed structured design, an application of the hierarchical principle to the relationships of the many small programs that, assembled into an intricate web of logic, constitute a software system.

To Yourdon, structured programming and design were just faster paths to disaster if the development team did not understand at the outset exactly what an internal client expected from the new software. In 1974, he and his wife, Toni Nash, founded the computer-consulting firm Yourdon, Inc., and by 1977 Yourdon had abandoned the teaching of structured programming and design to carry his vision of structured analysis into the software-development wilderness. A key assistant in this endeavor was to be Tom DeMarco, a systems analyst whom Yourdon had met a decade or so earlier. DeMarco gave form to the substance of Yourdon's ideas. He recognized that few human endeavors achieve perfect or even satisfactory results on the first try. "The idea," he wrote in a paper on structured analysis, "of developing a flawed early version and then refining and refining to make it right is a very old one. It is called engineering."

The vehicle for software engineering was to be the largely abandoned give-and-take between analyst and client. The practice, never strong, had deteriorated to the point, claimed DeMarco, "that instead of a meaningful interaction between analyst and user, there is often a period of fencing followed by the two parties' studiously ignoring each other." DeMarco envisioned continuous feedback from analyst to user—and vice versa—as plans for a new software system took shape. During the first stage of the process, in which the goal is to discover by interview how the client operates the business, the analyst would do little more than restate current practices to be certain that no misunderstanding passed unresolved.

As an aid to this procedure, DeMarco proposed the simple measure of writing each business operation and suboperation in a circle, or bubble, joined to other bubbles by arrows to indicate the sequence of processes and the flow of information through them. As the discussion proceeded, a second layer of bubbles and arrows would be drawn to record the substeps of the procedures outlined in the top level of bubbles. The process would continue, layer by layer, until a company's operations had been described in exhaustive detail. Then the process would begin anew, as the analyst undertook to describe how the new software would accomplish the same tasks—plus any others that the client might want in order to make the business run more smoothly. At each stage, the contents and workings of the system would be revised, gradually refining—or engineering—the proposal to the point where the analyst understood the needs of the client, who in turn was satisfied with the plan.

FORTUNES IN PENCILS AND ERASERS

Yourdon's and DeMarco's technique offered software developers a potent tool, albeit an imperfect one. Among its shortcomings was the time required to draw the bubbles, to position and label them, and to connect them with arrows. Rearranging elements of the design or adding new ones caused tedious redrawing. Each box of several on a page that represented a portion of a large program was accompanied by a second page of boxes itemizing the contents of the first box—and so on down to the finest specifics of the project.

The stack of paper representing the design could quickly grow to fill perhaps dozens of loose-leaf binders. Still more time was required to keep these files in perfect order and up-to-date; any lapse could make it impossible to compare related features of the design, leading to errors and inconsistencies that the process was intended to eliminate. In the words of a report on the state of software engineering, Yourdon-style diagramming was "usually abandoned just at the point where the rigor imposed by the method would have made a valuable contribution."

The solution to the drudgery had been obvious more than a decade earlier: Computerize the drawing of bubbles and lines. Doing this would make Yourdon diagrams easy to change, move about, and reconnect in different arrangements as analyst and user jostled toward a mutual understanding of the objective. Computers had for several years been providing similar services to engineers in other fields. The Boeing Company, for example, developed its own computer-assisted engineering (CAE) system. Using a high-powered work station connected to a mainframe computer, an aeronautical engineer might draw the shape of a plane's wing as glowing lines on the computer screen or perhaps describe the contours of the structure as equations, from which the software created an image of the airfoil. Supplied with other equations relating lift to airflow across the wing, the computer could simulate the airfoil's performance at different airspeeds. An unsatisfactory design could be easily altered and retested.

In this domain, flexibility, as well as savings in redrafting time and in costs of crafting scale models and testing them in a wind tunnel, more than compensated for the substantial amounts of expensive mainframe computer time required for this work. Comparable economics for similar reasons might have been possible in the world of software development. But most professionals in the field thought of themselves as artists more than engineers. By and large, they were unable to rationalize the expense of—or even see the value in—automating the analysis phase of their work.

RESOLVING THE HARDWARE BOTTLENECK

By 1983, however, the cost of computer time was no longer an issue. Powerful personal computers had become available. For a modest price by computing standards, they could be outfitted with the circuitry and monitors needed to produce colorful graphics, an essential ingredient for drawing data-flow diagrams. All manner of programs were written for these desktop machines, including some that addressed the front end of designing software.

Of those, a few were simply diagramming programs. The earliest of these software-development tools, actually written for use on a small minicomputer, was named Graphitext. Produced by the Nastec Corporation of Southfield, Michigan, in 1981, the product allowed a designer to draw Yourdon diagrams on the terminal screen and establish relationships between them. To John Manley, a vice president of Nastec, this brand-new approach to software development deserved a brand-new name—computer-aided software engineering. He called Graphitext a CASE tool.

During the following two years or so, Graphitext evolved into a more sophisticated tool kit that kept track of the relationships between diagram components in a multilayer database. Any bubble in a diagram could be opened up to reveal the relationships between the subordinate bubbles within—and so on, down to the most basic operations that the new software system was to perform. Graphitext also checked the analyst's work, making certain, for example, that every output from each element was channeled as input to an element that had been designed to receive it.

Other companies soon followed Nastec into the world of CASE. As software-engineering technology advanced, the tool kits became capable of producing prototypes having much the look and feel of the finished product. Before a line of code had been written, a client could try out the design. Any flaws could be quickly eliminated and retested (pages 38-49).

Early CASE software took a process-oriented approach to system analysis and design. That is, the analyst saw the job as one of first finding all the nooks and crannies of a data-processing operation and then tracking information step by step through the various stages. In this way, the analyst learned of the daily routine, as well as information required. However, software systems designed in this manner proved to be curiously narrow and inflexible. If a business altered its methods in some way and wished to have its software updated to reflect the new approach, likely as not there would be a data obstacle in the way. In some instances, information needed for the new software feature had not been identified as an important component of the original program when it was first developed. As a consequence, maintaining—that is, upgrading—old software became the single most time-consuming chore of programmers and analysts alike. Often forced to redesign a substantial portion of a software system almost from scratch, they spent as much as 80 percent of their time on these activities. With only one-fifth or so of programming resources available for new software, it is little wonder that delays in getting a project started often stretched on for years.

In 1976, Peter Chen, a professor at M.I.T., published an article entitled "Entity-Relationship Model: Toward a Unified View of Data." His paper would help change the way in which software developers viewed the business world. Chen had noted that the information an enterprise needs to operate—customer names, stock numbers, prices, personnel data, dates that orders are received and filled—remains remarkably constant. A study conducted of Washington State University's computerized records, for example, revealed that over a decade, between retiring unneeded data elements and adding new ones, the university's databases retained 80 percent of the original set. Yet during the same period of time, many new data-processing requirements emerged that combined all the data elements in different ways.

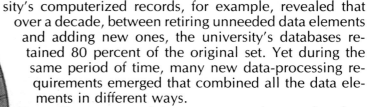

Chen proposed that systems analysts, rather than setting out to follow the crooked path of process, delve instead into the nature of the information fundamental to a user's business. The object was to understand the interrelationships between data elements, a process that Chen called data modeling. This would allow the construction of central databases containing all the information a company might wish to collate in various ways, some of them perhaps unimaginable at the time a new system is conceived. Furthermore, the databases were to be structured in a way that would make an easy job of adding new data elements or deleting outmoded ones. Once such a database had been built and loaded with information, the task of programming new uses of the information would be simplified. "Business algorithms are really very simple," says Greg Boone of the CASE Research Corporation, a market-research and consulting firm, consisting of little more than procedures for selecting appropriate information from the immense amount of data on file, sorting it, comparing it, updating it, and performing a limited repertoire of well-understood mathematical operations upon it.

LINKING FRONT END TO BACK END
The work of Chen, the academician, attracted the attention of James Martin, the computer iconoclast. Martin travels the world conducting three-day seminars on the future of data processing in the business world, serving as consultant—at the rate of $25,000 a day—to captains of industry and commerce, taping television workshops, and writing. Since 1963, he has published dozens of books about computers and computing.

Martin was born in Ashby-de-la-Zouch, a village in the English countryside bearing a name that commemorates the Norman conquest of England in the eleventh century. Shedding his "peasant roots," as he describes his early years, Martin took bachelor's and master's degrees in physics at Oxford University, and after military service he joined the British arm of International Business Machines. Sent to the United States in 1961, Martin contributed to one of the landmark programming projects of all time—SABRE, the innovative reservations network set up for American Airlines. On a later assignment, to IBM's office in London, he sold a similar system to BOAC (now British Airways), the largest order on record for that office.

That Martin, a technician and not one of the sales staff, snared the contract demonstrated a knack for explaining difficult computer science to laymen, a skill that he realized he could capitalize on. In 1977, having established a name for himself in a variety of computer specialties—communications and database management among them—Martin took a year's sabbatical from IBM to begin conducting the seminars that would make him wealthy. His income for the year exceeded that of IBM's president, John Opel. "I was surprised," he said some years later, "that it was possible to make that amount of money." He never returned to IBM.

In 1979, Martin founded a company called Database Design, Inc. Renamed KnowledgeWare a few years later, the purpose of the venture was to develop a CASE product based in part on Chen's ideas of data modeling. In a business context, the entities that Chen wrote of are records in a database of everything that plays a role in, say, manufacturing a product and selling it—sales and work orders, contracts, suppliers, invoices, and inventory, to name but a few.

In Martin's opinion, front-end CASE tools, though helpful, were far from a complete set of software-engineering programs. He envisioned an integrated system that would take the software-development process from beginning to end, starting with planning, analysis, and design, and ending with fully functioning programs. Searching for a supplier of back-end features, Martin eventually turned to an Atlanta company, Tarkenton Software, Inc. Founded by football quarterback Fran Tarkenton, the company had already developed an application generator—software that produces code from a detailed design—when sports star met computer guru in 1986. "We're both hard-driving guys," Tarkenton says, "and we hit it off right away." Tarkenton Software merged with KnowledgeWare later that year, and their collaboration bore fruit in 1988 in the form of a fully integrated CASE system called Information Engineering Workbench. Front-end analyis and back-end code generation were at last combined in a single, unified product.

By this time, others had come to appreciate the benefits of the data-modeling approach to the design of CASE systems intended for business-software development. For example, Bachman Information Systems in Cambridge, Massachusetts, had been hard at work on their version of a data-oriented, integrated CASE system called the Bachman Re-Engineering Product Set. In nearby Waltham, the Cortex Corporation had CorVision underway, also a front-end-to-back-end system—the very software that had come to the rescue of Herman Nichols and East Bay Water. And Texas Instruments had begun the design of an integrated system the company called the Information Engineering Facility, or IEF.

2

Well aware through James Martin's seminars of his groundwork on the data-modeling approach to software analysis, Texas Instruments in 1983 sought Martin's assistance in helping to design an in-house CASE system. TI wished to follow up on Martin's advice the preceding year to members of the company's board of directors that the company improve its software-development technology. Five years later, IEF was ready not only for TI's own use, but for sale to other companies as well. The Texas Instruments CASE system consists of five sections, intended to be used in sequence, that TI calls toolsets.

First in line is a planning toolset for a preanalysis phase in which a software developer confers with a business's leadership. Proponents of information engineering—and James Martin in particular—urge that a company's topmost managers participate in this stage. Their broad view of the company and its operations, both present and future, helps to assure completeness of the database on which new software will depend. The objective is to describe the company in terms of its component activities or functions—contracting, purchasing, order processing, vehicle maintenance, scrap disposal, and the like—and the information needed to conduct the business and monitor its progress—sales, work,

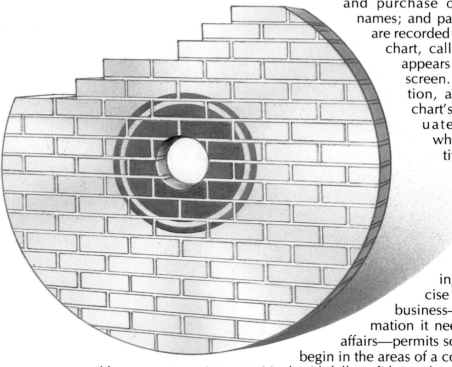

and purchase orders; customer names; and payments. Activities are recorded across the top of a chart, called a matrix, that appears on the computer screen. Types of information, arrayed down the chart's left side, are evaluated to establish which company activities need access to each kind of information and which operations are responsible for originating, updating, and deleting data. This concise picture of an entire business—and of the information it needs to conduct its affairs—permits software analysis to begin in the areas of a company where the need for new systems is most critical, with full confidence that the work will mesh with systems created later for other departments.

Next, IEF's analysis tool is used to produce both data- and activity-modeling diagrams that show in detail the relationships between a department and the relevant data elements from the matrix. This tool is also used to establish sequences of events. For example, a shipment of supplies arriving by truck at a warehouse might be tracked through three steps before the order is recorded as filled: a notation that the goods were signed over by the truckdriver; a subsequent remark that the shipment had been inspected; and finally, an entry that indicates whether the materials were accepted as satisfactory or judged defective and returned to the supplier.

Using IEF's design tool, an analyst next spells out the principles embodied in the data-flow diagrams as statements in a design language, built into the CASE software, that express the logic of the program—that is, the steps it will take to accomplish the tasks envisioned for it. The results of this phase permit IEF to display a prototype of the new software for evaluation. They also constitute the raw material for the following two stages of the software-development process— the automatic generation of computer code in COBOL, an old but still-popular business-programming language, and the automatic creation of the databases that will hold the information identified in the earliest phases of the project.

PROMISE UNFULFILLED

Judging from the enthusiasm for Texas Instruments' integrated toolkit at Touche-Ross, a large accounting firm, and at Scott Paper Company, and from the availability of similar products by KnowledgeWare, Bachman Information Systems, and CorVision, CASE appears to have indeed delivered a method of engineering software that substantially reduces the cost of new software and the time needed to write it. Yet there has been no rush to embrace the technology, and for several reasons.

First, it is new. Business executives have been disappointed in the past by glossy promises of a bright new world that lay just beyond the gateway of computerization. Now they are suspicious of every claim. Even with CASE, developing a new software system can take a very long time indeed. James Martin estimates that the initial planning phase with a company's top management may stretch at least three months and perhaps as long as a year. Analysis of individual divisions or departments may last six months longer, depending on the scope of the operations involved. Design and construction—that is, writing the software in a CASE language, and generating code and databases—can require as little as a few weeks or may extend over a period of years, according to system complexity. On the surface, CASE seems to make little improvement in the rate at which new systems can be developed. In rebuttal, CASE advocates contend that the software, when at last delivered, will function as intended. Furthermore, because a CASE design is easy to modify in response to changing circumstances, the final product will address the client's current needs, not an obsolete set of specifications. The CASE approach also makes programs so much easier to maintain that the time devoted to upgrading them as they become obsolete may be reduced by half or more.

Such efficiencies are also offered in answer to the objection that CASE is expensive. When TI's Information Engineering Facility first became available, the automatic COBOL and database generators, which ran only on a main-frame, cost more than a quarter of a million dollars. For the planning, analysis, and design toolsets combined, the company charged nearly $14,000 per copy. Additionally, there was the price of a personal computer to consider. Because CASE depends on computer graphics for drawing data-modeling diagrams, a more expensive machine is needed than the kind demanded by the word-processing software traditionally used for programming, and the combined cost of software and hardware approached $22,000 per desk. For a shop of 200 analysts and programmers, the investment exceeds $4 million, and Yourdon points out that the costs of training, hardware maintenance, and other incidentals can easily cause the bill for CASE during the first five years to top $6 million. In any endeavor, such an expensive tool would receive close scrutiny for cost-effectiveness.

The lack of a reliable way to forecast or even to measure increases in productivity that might result from spending money on CASE has made businesses doubly cautious. Typically, a pilot project is established to determine by experience whether—and by how much—CASE speeds the work. Given that a single software-development effort might take months or even years to complete, the evaluation period for new technology is a lengthy one.

Even if CASE proves valuable in a small-scale test, many hurdles remain to wider use. Taking the drudgery out of data-model diagramming by having the computer do the drawing, erasing, and redrawing does not address the fundamental resistance of a great many programmers and systems analysts to the idea of planning ahead in full and fine detail. The mechanical engineer's approach to problem solving, in which the solution is constructed only after the length and diameter of every bolt has been specified and the design has been thoroughly examined by computer simulation, is in large measure alien to them. Programmers and analysts with this point of view regard CASE—along with many of the tools that preceded it—as a threat to their accustomed way of doing things. ''They fight them tooth and nail,'' says Webber.

Strong leadership at the top of an organization can make a difference. But in many companies, the salaries of software-development managers depend in part on the number of people they have working for them. If CASE were to increase productivity by, say, 50 percent, the programming staff might well be reduced, diminishing the manager's influence. Even those inclined to establish new software-development procedures despite the possibility of seeing their own budgets shrink often procrastinate for fear of driving their programmers and analysts to seek employment with another, more lenient employer. And the risk is appreciable, because programmers change jobs often. In most fields, a succession of five jobs in seven years would raise questions about an individual's professional character; in the software industry, however, such job-hopping is the norm. In addition, many managers are sympathetic with the programmers and analysts, often having graduated from the same work themselves. They are thus ill-prepared to impose a radically different regime on the people working for them.

SKEPTICISM IN THE BOARDROOM

Even in the best of circumstances, CASE is often a hard sell. At American Telephone & Telegraph in 1985, in the wake of the court-ordered divestiture that split up the once-monolithic communications giant into smaller companies, the army of analysts and programmers responsible for working up new software systems for the corporation were inundated. More systems had to be produced in less time with fewer people than ever before. Morale was sagging. Clearly, some remedy was needed, and quickly.

Particularly under the gun was Barbara Bouldin, working at AT&T Information Systems in Parsippany, New Jersey. She was staff manager for order-processing systems, the software that keeps track of customer requests for new service and equipment. AT&T-IS was already well committed to the principles of structured analysis in software design when Bouldin approached her own boss, Thomas Cooper, about the seeming impossibility of meeting the demand for software. Since the mid-1970s, Cooper had dreamed of creating a system of software tools that would tame the front end of the software development process. Said Cooper: "We were seeing a lot of problems coming from information structured in multiple ways." A single data element—an order number, for example—might have a different name in as many as thirty-five programs. Inasmuch as CASE promises to eliminate such confusion by vastly improving coordination between programmers working on projects that share information, the towering workload at AT&T-IS seemed to offer Cooper a golden opportunity.

Cooper first investigated the possibility of diverting resources to the task of creating a CASE tool kit, but "it got to be too much." He recalled, "We wanted a Rolls Royce." He then surveyed the field of ready-to-use packages, settling on one called Excelerator by Index Technology Corporation. It seemed to satisfy most of their requirements and appeared to be maturing in a direction that would fulfill others. Cooper recognized that learning the new software would be viewed by Bouldin's programmers as little more than an added chore at a time when they were already overburdened. To succeed, Bouldin would have to display the zeal of a missionary on a crusade.

She began with "a marketing blitz," demonstrating the software to whomever she could buttonhole for a few minutes. She probed the staff to discover their doubts about the CASE tools and to understand how she might make it attractive to them. A task force formed to implement the new system decided under Bouldin's guidance to start with something simple—compiling a data dictionary from existing AT&T-IS software to alleviate the problem of multiple names for identical data elements. Such inconsistency is a common cause of software failure. Within a few months the data dictionary was ready, and within a short time thereafter, said Bouldin, "I was hearing the organization say the data dictionary was the official source, and that was the moment I knew we had changed things."

Although the new CASE tools were not fully integrated with each other, a survey of the staff revealed a high degree of satisfaction with the new approach— 100 percent among software designers, for example. Spreading through Bouldin's operation, the tools gradually made a difference. The flood of requests for software became more manageable. Morale improved. Her customers were more pleased than ever, pleased at the opportunity to help tailor a software design to their particular requirements.

At AT&T Information Management Services in Piscataway, New Jersey, Duane Luse oversees the activities of 1,800 analysts and programmers. With nearly thirty years' experience in the software-development business, Luse long ago became a skeptic in the matter of ending or even shrinking the software backlog. "Every time a new thing's announced," he says, "it's nirvana. I have been through almost all of those, and they have never panned out." Yet even he is guardedly hopeful about CASE: "I think this time we may possibly have a breakthrough." In Luse's view, software development staffs will be induced to adopt a structured-analysis approach to their profession, not by their own managers, but by the company clients they serve. Seeing that CASE can speed the programming process, business managers thirsting for new software seem more than willing to acquire working knowledge of a diagramming language in order to take earlier delivery of software that is also more reliable.

Among the more exciting prospects of the CASE system Luse has selected for AT&T—the Bachman Re-Engineering Product Set—is the software's ability to subject COBOL code produced by traditional programming methods to a process called reverse engineering. Assisted by a human analyst or programmer, the Bachman Product dissects old programs and restructures them according to data-modeling principles. With this facility, the Bachman software promises to bring the benefits of lower maintenance costs not only to new computer applications, but to the billions of lines of existing software as well.

A GUARDED PROGNOSIS

The future of CASE is hazy. Luse predicts a quiet revolution, in which an irresistible tide of consumer demand for the new way of building software simply carries away those who resist. Others feel that a full flowering of CASE awaits a new generation of developers, brought up in the wisdom and practice of the new modus operandi.

Similar evolution has occurred in other engineering disciplines. A century or so ago, bridge builders worked in haphazard, trial-and-error fashion. The resulting structure might stand for decades—or it might fail at the first overloaded wagon. Gradually, civil engineering became more science than art, with certification procedures to assure the bridge-buying public that the designers knew their business. Some observers of the software scene predict: If the structured-analysis approach to software development ever demonstrates conclusively that it produces better results more cheaply than the programmer-as-artist method, consumers of custom software will ultimately expect suppliers to be licensed experts in the practice of structured analysis.

Yourdon anticipates that independent software developers "are likely to begin developing generic CASE 'templates' for common applications." Templates are customizations of generic software for personal computers written by enterprising programmers to save less-knowledgeable owners of these machines the time and frustration of doing the work themselves. For example, templates are available for spreadsheet programs that run on personal computers to convert the blank rows and columns into worksheets for every purpose, from calculating income tax to complex statistical analysis. Such a template can be used as is or revised by the user as necessary. In the same spirit, independent systems analysts might construct for CASE systems templates that set up structures for a variety of business activities. "Thus, if a user wants to build a payroll system," says Yourdon, "he might buy a ready-made set of data-flow diagrams, a data dictionary, and all the rest for a modest amount of money. Then he could customize that template, using his CASE work station, to produce a complete specification for the system he wants."

Perhaps on the farthest horizon, CASE may make a software developer of virtually anyone. In another arena, microcomputer database programs, once all but impenetrable to people who did not belong to the fellowship of programmers, have been given the ability to make sense of queries expressed in everyday English. If the program cannot relate the question to the information in the database—a request for a sales total by region, for example, when the database keeps the figure by district—it quizzes the user to establish the correct relationship between the question and the available data, then remembers the connection for the next occasion. CASE tools, given a similar capability to understand plain English instead of yet another arcane computer language, might make it possible for a business manager to become a master of software, to take over the design of all but the largest systems.

Programming in Pieces

Computers have long been used to simulate events in the real world, from battlefield encounters and global weather patterns to all sorts of production processes. Such simulations can serve a variety of purposes. Computerized combat may yield tactical or strategic insights, for example; a production-line simulation may reveal inefficiencies and indicate ways to get rid of them. But traditional sequential programming does not always lend itself readily to this sort of job. With its series of step-by-step instructions typically linked together as an integral unit, such software can be a difficult medium to work in, especially when it comes to making adjustments in a simulation; altering a single factor sometimes requires re-working much of the program.

Object-oriented programming, a relatively recent addition to the ranks of programming techniques, offers an attractive alternative. It accommodates the fact that people tend to perceive the world in terms of objects, which may interact with one another but are nonetheless identifiable as independent entities. Thus, instead of a continuous stream of instructions, object-oriented programs organize data and procedures into small chunks called objects, each of which represents a discrete element or aspect of the situation being simulated. These program chunks can be assembled, disassembled, and rearranged by the programmer like building blocks, and each can be tested or adjusted separately, making a large and complex program far easier to write and debug than it would be if written in the conventional way. Objects can also be lifted from one program and used in another with little or no modification.

Since the early 1980s, dozens of object-oriented programming techniques have been developed. The following pages illustrate some of them in an imaginary context—simulating the steps in a pizza-making operation to achieve the optimal production process.

Assembly-line pizza. The diagram below illustrates one possible arrangement of work stations for a high-volume pizza kitchen. Stations are connected by delivery chutes that forward pizzas from one station to the next. Some tasks, such as adding cheese and baking the pies, are assigned to more than one station in an effort to maintain an efficient flow of pizzas through the system.

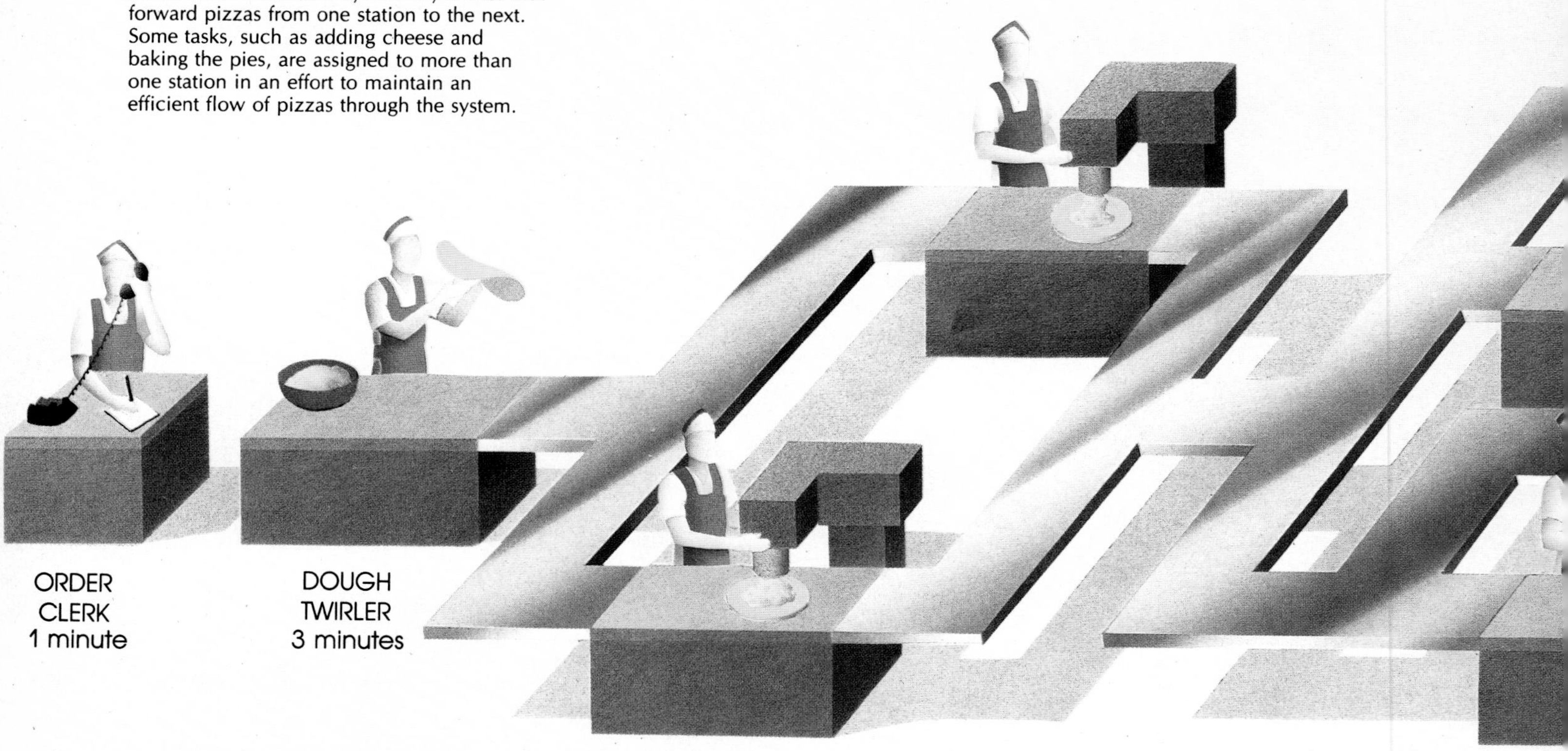

ORDER
CLERK
1 minute

DOUGH
TWIRLER
3 minutes

CHEESIFIERS
5 minutes

PEPPERONIST/MUSHROOMER
7 minutes each

Building Blocks for a Production Line

Assembly-line production, whether for something as complex as computer chips or as simple as pizzas, depends on the coordination of a series of distinct tasks. Determining the best procedure is seldom as straightforward as it seems. The slightest miscalculation can tip the balance between a system that runs smoothly and one that suffers costly delays.

The design of the imaginary pizza kitchen above began with a step-by-step outlining of the various tasks involved in making a pizza, each represented by a particular type of work station. The precise arrangement of stations is based on the assumption that producing a pizza every four minutes will

satisfy peak demand; to meet this goal, no step in the process can take longer than an average of four minutes. By including two stations for adding cheese and three for baking, the production-line designer figures to keep the average working time for those steps below four minutes.

A further estimate, founded on research into the business, steers the designer away from adding extra stations for the seven-minute pepperoni or mushroom stages. If it is assumed that the four kinds of pizza (opposite) will be ordered in roughly equal numbers, then only half the orders—for pepperoni and for "the works" (every possible topping)—require the services of the pepperonist, and that station's average working time is cut in half; the same holds true for the mushroomer. Such logic and educated guesswork may well lead to the most efficient arrangement of components. But by simulating the process on a computer, the production-line designer can make sure.

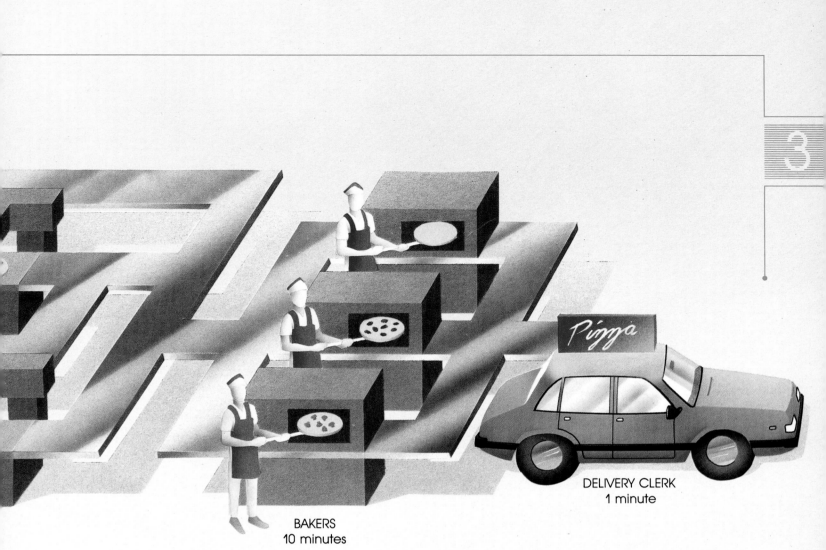

BAKERS
10 minutes

DELIVERY CLERK
1 minute

A MATTER OF TIMING

Four kinds of pizza are made by the production line pictured above, and each takes a different amount of time, depending on the toppings it requires. A plain cheese pizza, which goes through only five stations, takes twenty minutes. A "works" pizza needs fourteen minutes more, spending seven minutes each at the pepperonist and the mushroomer. The times listed at right apply only if each station is available whenever a pizza reaches it; in reality, backups can occur where shorter tasks precede longer ones.

CHEESE	$1 + 3 + 5 + 10 + 1 = 20$
PEPPERONI	$1 + 3 + 5 + 7 + 10 + 1 = 27$
MUSHROOM	$1 + 3 + 5 + 7 + 10 + 1 = 27$
THE WORKS	$1 + 3 + 5 + 7 + 7 + 10 + 1 = 34$

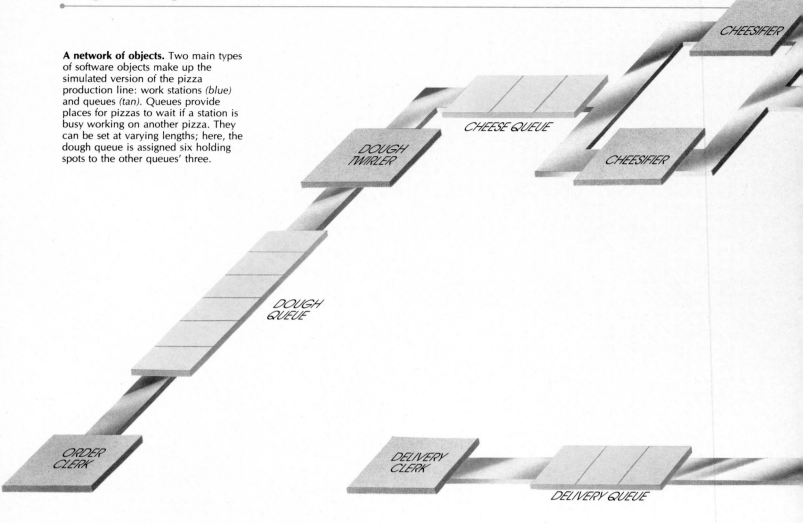

A network of objects. Two main types of software objects make up the simulated version of the pizza production line: work stations *(blue)* and queues *(tan)*. Queues provide places for pizzas to wait if a station is busy working on another pizza. They can be set at varying lengths; here, the dough queue is assigned six holding spots to the other queues' three.

Software Objects That Simulate Action

To determine if the pizza kitchen's design will work efficiently, a program is created to mimic the behavior of the actual system. Object-oriented programming is an ideal medium for such a simulation because its software objects—the independent program chunks of which it is composed—function together in much the same way as the real-life components of the kitchen. The computer's objects can be rearranged, modified, or duplicated just like the individual work stations and other elements of the pizza assembly line.

The first step in designing the simulation program is to identify what types, or classes, of objects will be needed.

Commercial object-programming packages typically provide a selection of ready-made object classes grouped in family trees according to shared characteristics *(right)*. For a given type of component—such as the queues between work stations—the programmer searches through a hierarchy of more and more narrowly defined classes to find the one whose characteristics best match the desired design feature, then uses it as a prototype for producing the requisite number of specific objects.

Programmers can generate their own hierarchies or extend existing ones with ease because of a principle known as inheritance. Whenever an object is created, it inherits all the characteristics of its parent, distinguishing itself only by the inclusion of any additional features. Thus the programmer can readily develop new types of objects without having to start over from scratch every time with a whole new set of computer code.

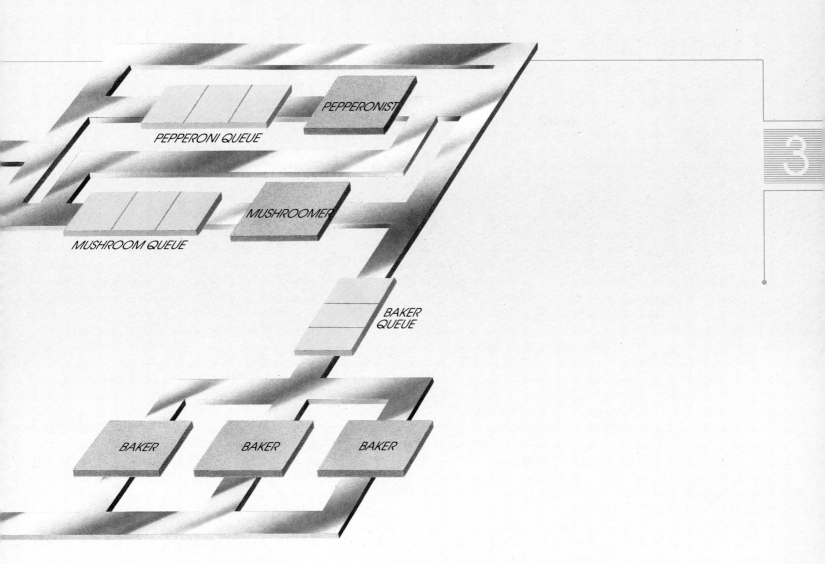

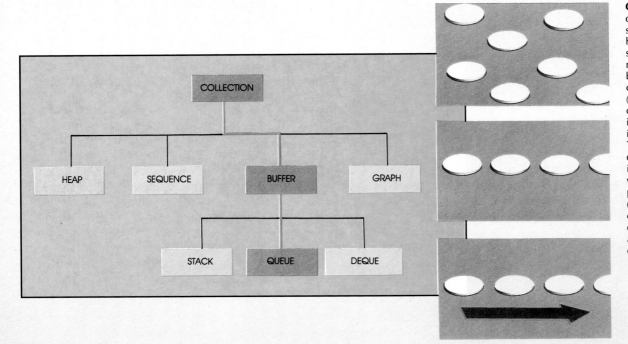

Queue genealogy. Queues are one of several related types of software objects linked in a hierarchy of progressively more specialized classes *(far left)*. The most general class is a collection, broadly defined as any object capable of storing multiple items *(near left, top)*. Four subclasses of collection specify how stored items are organized; buffers impose a linear order *(middle)*. The three buffer subclasses define different methods of retrieving items: in a stack, the first item in will be the last out; a queue passes items straight through *(arrow, bottom),* so that the first one in is the first out; a double-ended queue, or deque, allows items to be removed from either end of the line.

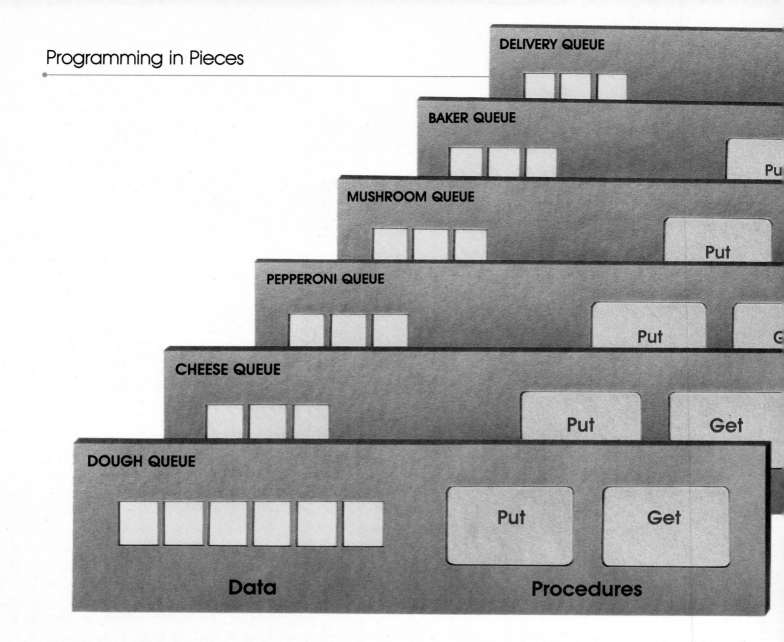

DELIVERY QUEUE

BAKER QUEUE Pu

MUSHROOM QUEUE Put

PEPPERONI QUEUE Put G

CHEESE QUEUE Put Get

DOUGH QUEUE

Data   Put   Get   Procedures

Program Specifics of an Object's Makeup

To exist as an independent entity, every object in a program must itself be a miniature program, complete with all the information and instructions it needs to perform its specified functions. Since objects incorporate the procedures and data that define their class, a minimal amount of additional information or fine-tuning of instructions usually suffices to get each object in working order. The class definition for queues, for example, represents queue length with a variable; as each individual queue object is created, the programmer assigns a specific value to that variable to ensure that the queue will hold precisely as many items as the design intends.

Objects must also be able to interact with one another if they are to simulate a working process. They do so by exchanging messages, each of which is directed toward and activates a specific procedure detailed within another object's programming.

At the same time, message sending helps ensure object independence because there are no permanent links written into the fabric of the program, as there might be in more traditional sequential programming; altering or even removing an object has no effect on other objects, so long as the messages they need are supplied.

The two procedures indicated above, to "put" items into a queue and to "get" them out, represent only the surface layer of what a queue object can do. Other skills are passed on from parent classes. The ability to keep track of space available, for instance, is inherent in every object that can trace its origin to the collection class.

A complement of queues. Each of the six queue objects needed for the pizza kitchen simulation embodies the same basic features established in the class definition of queues. Queue size, represented at left by rows of small boxes, varies from six for the dough queue to three for all the others. The boxes labeled Put and Get represent the programmed set of instructions that spell out in detail how items are put into the proper place in line and what happens when a message is received to get an item out of the queue.

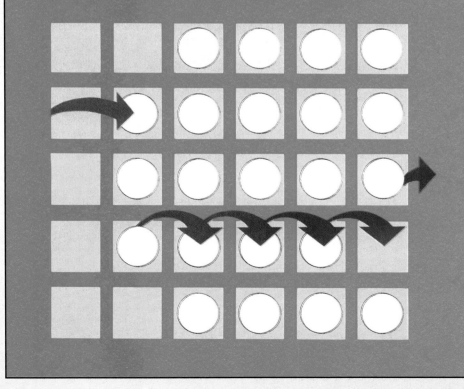

INS AND OUTS OF A QUEUE

Although the logic of how items move through a queue—so that the first one in will be the first one out—is readily apparent to the human mind, a programmer must be sure that every queue object includes step-by-step instructions to be followed in manipulating stored items. The five diagrams below of a six-place queue illustrate some of the details involved. The four items already present have been assigned to the four rightmost spots, ready to be removed in order from the right-hand end of the queue. When the queue receives a "put" message, it adds an item by skipping the leftmost spot and filling the farthest open spot to the right. A "get" message leads not only to the removal of the rightmost item but to the shifting of every stored item one place to the right; thus, five separate actions are necessary to prepare the queue once again for adding or removing items in the proper sequence.

Getting the Message Across

In addition to the messages that invoke procedures, objects also exchange status information that helps determine the course of events and reveals how efficiently the simulated system is running. For instance, before a work station can forward a pizza to the next queue, it must find out if that queue is already full. If a message from the queue indicates that it is, the station has no choice but to stop working and wait until space is available.

Status messages from queues are relatively simple. In response to a "put" message from a preceding work station, a queue either initiates the procedure for adding an item or sends a "full" message back to the station; a "get" message from a succeeding station prompts either the removal of an item from the queue or the forwarding of an "empty" message. Work stations, however, must be able to report four different states: a station in the midst of a task is "working"; when it has just sent a pizza to the next queue, it is "available"; when it has completed a task but a full queue prevents it from beginning another, it is "blocked"; and when a supplying queue is empty, the station is "starved."

Since the timing of various tasks is a key design feature, an effective simulation must be able to track these object states over time. In the example on these pages, one station's changing status is followed through fifteen time-steps, each of which represents either one minute of the station's working time or an exchange of messages between objects.

Work-station status. The chart below and opposite shows how the status of the dough-twirler station changes through four color-coded states as it interacts with the dough queue and the cheese queue *(right)*. Pizzas are labeled C, P, M, or W ("the works") to indicate which toppings they require. For clarity, only three of the dough queue's six holding spots are included.

WORKING

AVAILABLE

BLOCKED

STARVED

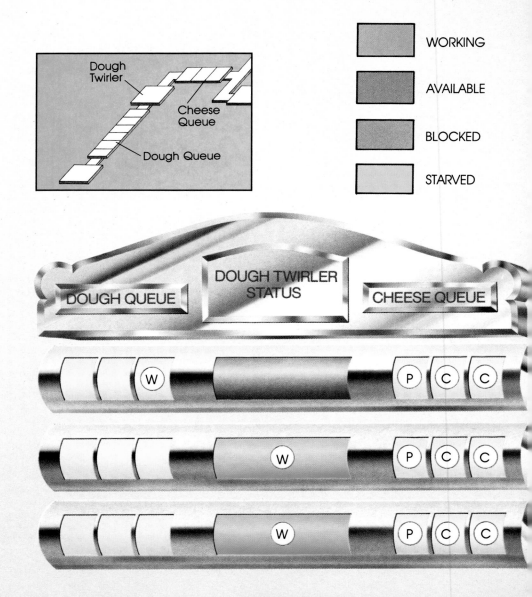

Currently available *(blue)*, the twirler sends a "get" message to the dough queue, asking it to forward a pizza.

The dough twirler receives a works pizza (W) from the dough queue and changes its status to green: working.

During this and the next time-step *(opposite, top)*, the dough twirler continues to work on its task, which requires a total of three time-steps. The twirler passes no messages until its task is completed.

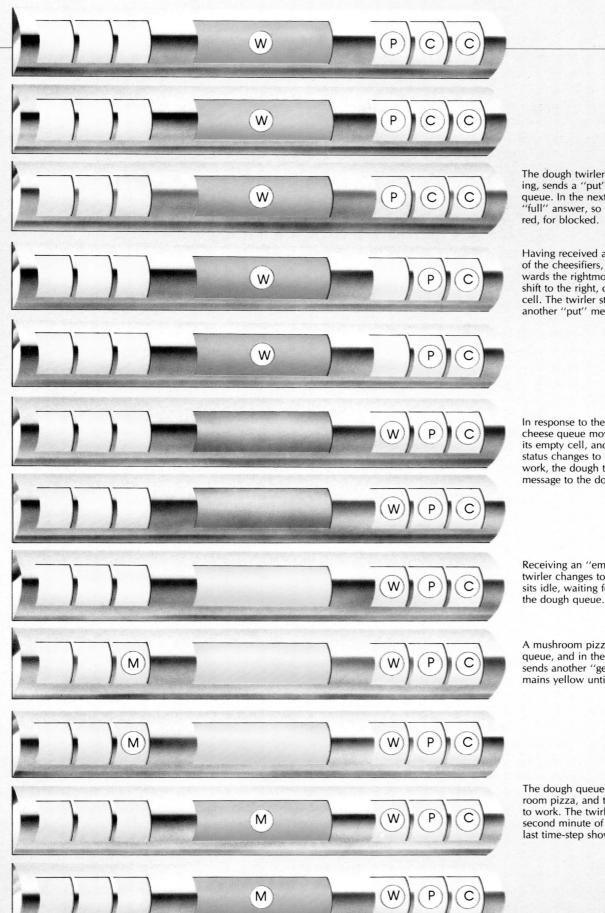

The dough twirler, still labeled as working, sends a "put" message to the cheese queue. In the next step, it gets back a "full" answer, so its status changes to red, for blocked.

Having received a "get" message from one of the cheesifiers, the cheese queue forwards the rightmost pizza; the other two shift to the right, opening a space in the last cell. The twirler stays blocked as it sends another "put" message during the next step.

In response to the "put" message, the cheese queue moves the works pizza into its empty cell, and the dough twirler's status changes to blue. Looking for more work, the dough twirler sends a "get" message to the dough queue (below).

Receiving an "empty" message, the dough twirler changes to yellow, for starved. It sits idle, waiting for a pizza to appear in the dough queue.

A mushroom pizza appears in the dough queue, and in the next step the twirler sends another "get" message; its status remains yellow until an answer is received.

The dough queue forwards its mushroom pizza, and the dough twirler gets to work. The twirler continues into a second minute of working time in the last time-step shown.

Objects in action. Arrows in the diagram at right indicate multiple actions taking place during a single time-step in the running of the simulation. As the order clerk puts a pizza in the dough queue, the top cheesifier sends a mushroom pizza to the mushroom queue and the bottom cheesifier sends a cheese pizza directly to the baker queue; at the same time, one of the bakers, having finished its work, forwards a pizza to the delivery clerk.

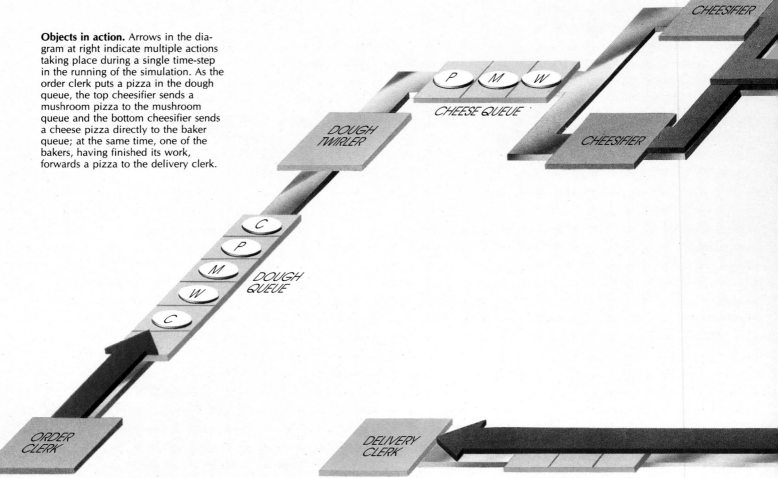

Spotting Trouble in the System Design

Once all the objects have been properly assembled into a program that simulates the entire pizza kitchen, the arrangement can be put through its paces to determine efficiency. The simulation commences with the object representing the first work station—the order clerk—being fed data representing the arrival of orders. As the program runs, messages fly between objects, and work stations change from state to state, all to mimic the progress, or lack thereof, of pizzas through the assembly line.

In order to discover any problem areas in the system's design, the program must be able to monitor the condition of every object throughout the simulation, which may run for as many as one thousand time-steps. The task can become quite complex and may, in some cases, call for sophisticated statistical analysis to detect flow patterns. The grid at far right illustrates in simplified form how this sort of tracking might be accomplished, with color-coded squares to show the status of each work station at successive time-steps. Patterns of blocked or starved stations indicate where the system is working at less than ideal efficiency.

The trouble appears to be related to the pepperonist and the mushroomer. The pepperonist has to sit idle for eight time-steps waiting for the mushroomer to finish its task and get another pizza, thereby opening a space in the mushroom queue. Before long, the delay starts blocking other work stations upstream and starving stations downstream.

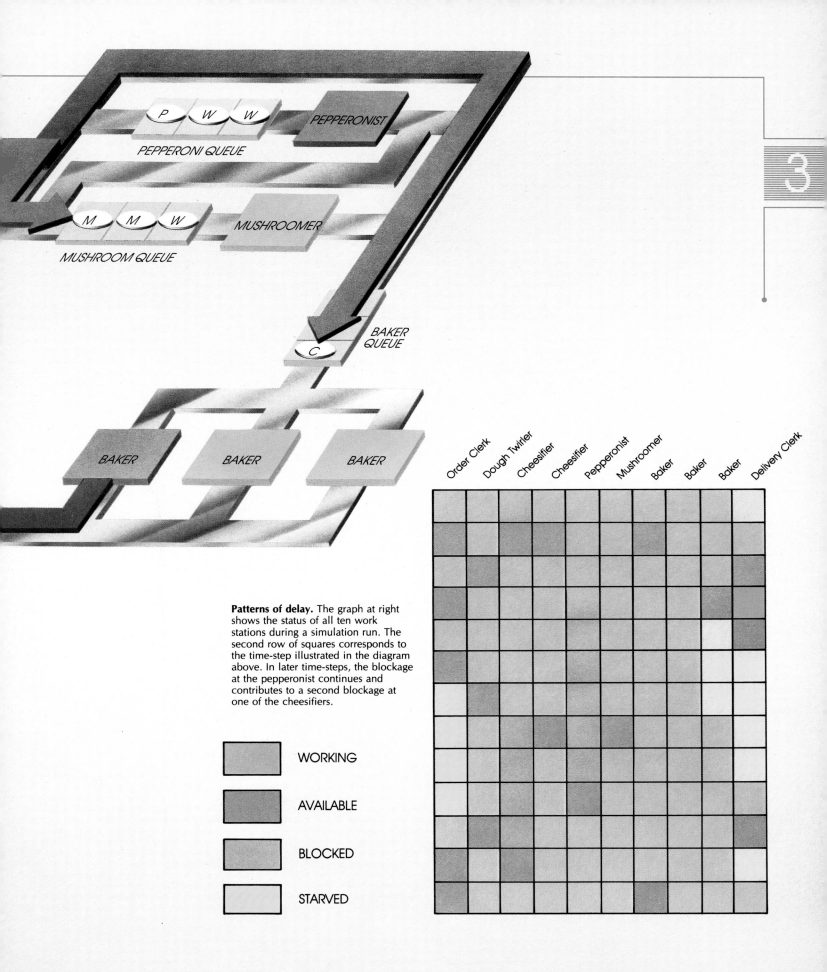

PEPPERONI QUEUE

PEPPERONIST

MUSHROOM QUEUE

MUSHROOMER

BAKER QUEUE

BAKER   BAKER   BAKER

Patterns of delay. The graph at right
shows the status of all ten work
stations during a simulation run. The
second row of squares corresponds to
the time-step illustrated in the diagram
above. In later time-steps, the blockage
at the pepperonist continues and
contributes to a second blockage at
one of the cheesifiers.

WORKING

AVAILABLE

BLOCKED

STARVED

Order Clerk   Dough Twirler   Cheesifier   Cheesifier   Pepperonist   Mushroomer   Baker   Baker   Baker   Delivery Clerk

Lengthening queues. The color coding of work stations in the diagram at right demonstrates the positive effects of modifying the pepperoni and mushroom queues to hold six pizzas apiece. Although both new queues are full during this particular time-step, no work station is blocked, indicating that the system is currently handling the flow of work efficiently.

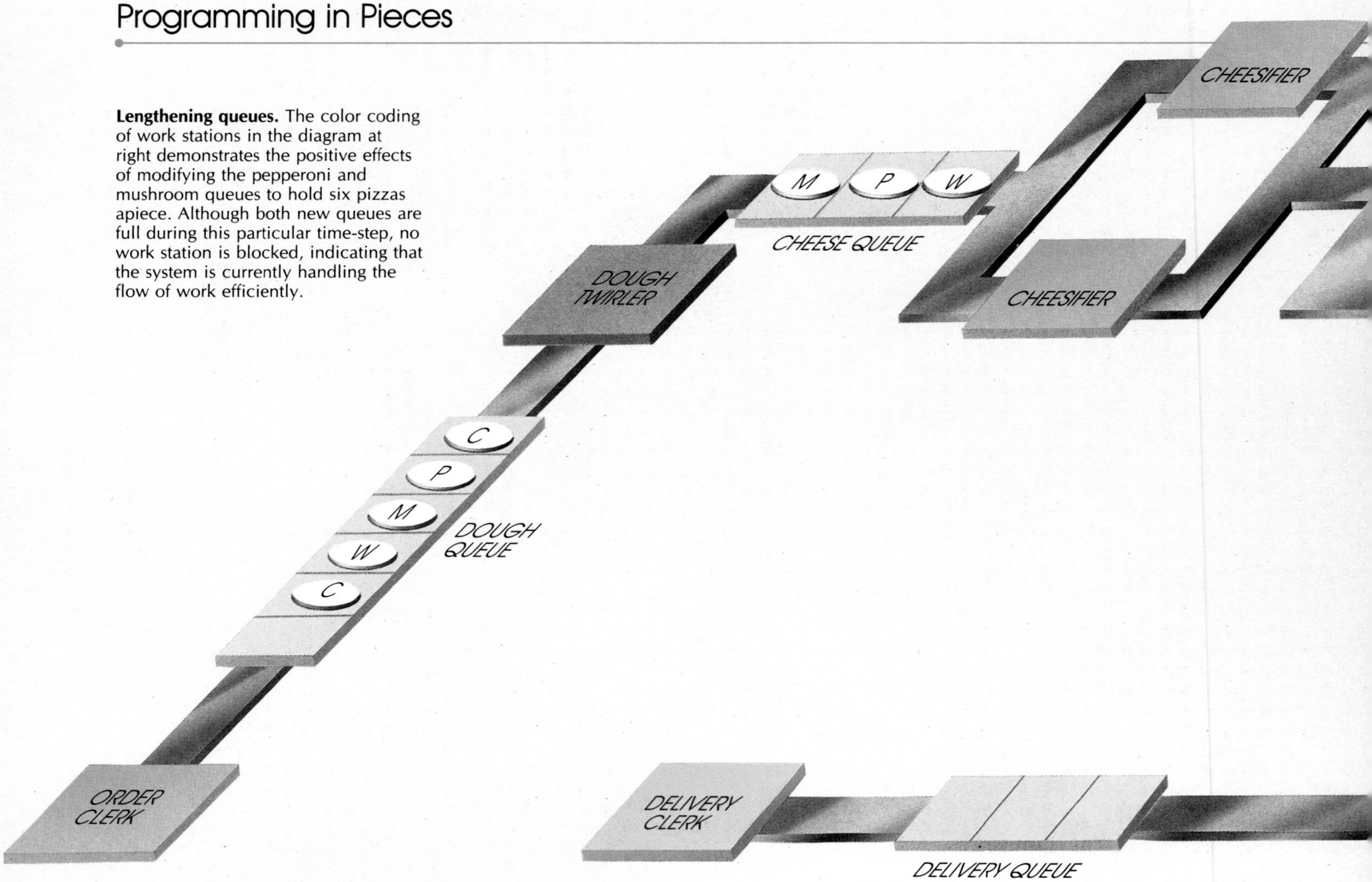

An Easily Tested Alternative Plan

Even when a specific problem area has been identified, the appropriate corrective action is not always readily apparent. Sometimes a designer may wish to consider several new approaches. An object-oriented program makes it easy to test such alternatives with full-scale simulation runs. In the example here, one possible solution to the pepperoni bottleneck might be to add another mushroomer, easily accomplished in the simulation by creating a duplicate mushroom object and linking it into the program. Another approach,

illustrated above, would be to lengthen both the mushroom queue, which has been blocking the pepperonist, and the pepperoni queue, which has been blocking one of the cheesifiers. Again, the adjustment is made in a small portion of the simulation with minimal disruption to the rest of the program; the length variable for the two queue objects is simply changed from three to six.

The designer must, of course, keep a number of factors in mind, besides what the simulation reveals, before making a final determination of the best approach. For instance, although adding another work station might prove more effective in the testing, longer queues would clearly be less costly to implement in the real-world system. But object-oriented programming unquestionably facilitates matters by providing a ready means for testing a wide variety of possibilities.

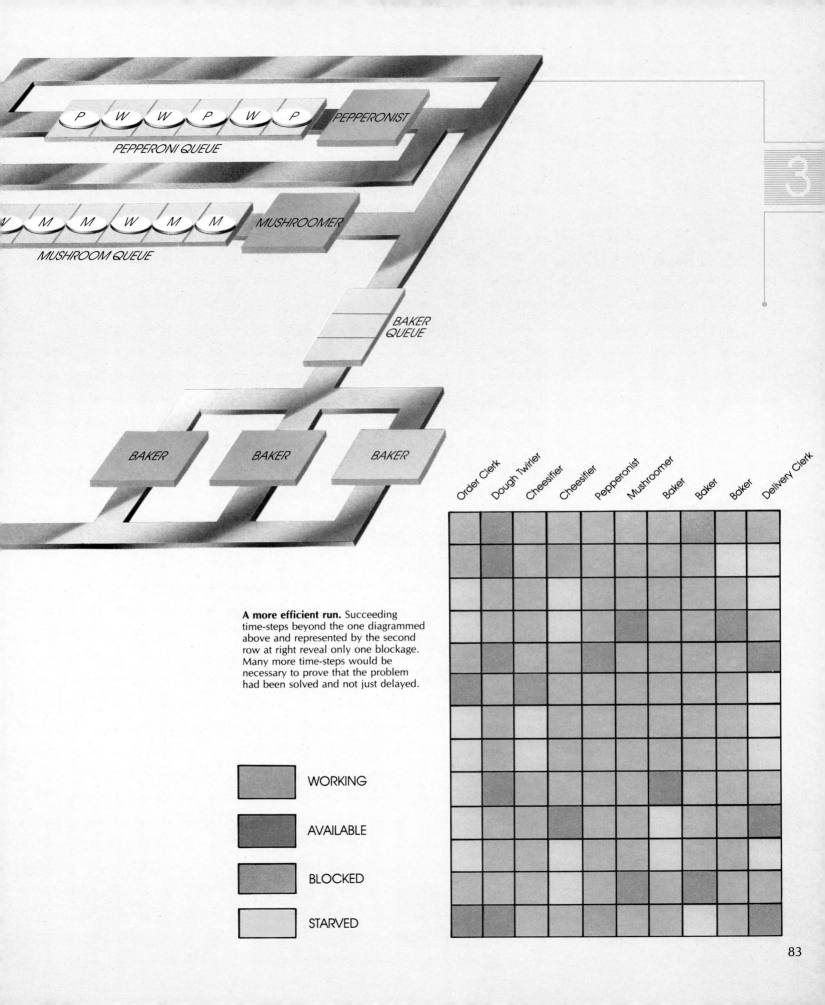

PEPPERONIST

PEPPERONI QUEUE

MUSHROOMER

MUSHROOM QUEUE

BAKER
QUEUE

BAKER   BAKER   BAKER

A more efficient run. Succeeding
time-steps beyond the one diagrammed
above and represented by the second
row at right reveal only one blockage.
Many more time-steps would be
necessary to prove that the problem
had been solved and not just delayed.

WORKING

AVAILABLE

BLOCKED

STARVED

Order Clerk · Dough Twirler · Cheesifier · Cheesifier · Pepperonist · Mushroomer · Baker · Baker · Baker · Delivery Clerk

Slashing the
Gordian Knot

3

Assembled in Seattle in the fall of 1977 for the annual conference of the Association for Computing Machinery (ACM), programmers, hardware designers, and computer-industry executives paused, as was their custom, to honor one of their own. The man of the hour was John Backus, a luminous figure in the history of computing. During the 1950s, Backus had headed a small IBM team that developed FORTRAN, one of the first and most successful of the high-level programming languages. His team also provided an essential adjunct—software called a compiler to translate the new dialect into one that IBM computers of the era could understand. Twenty years later, though the industry had seen the introduction of dozens of other, more advanced languages, FORTRAN was still widely used (as it is to this day).

In recognition of FORTRAN and other significant contributions to the software craft, the ACM had bestowed upon Backus the much-coveted Turing Award, named for Alan M. Turing, designer of Britain's first electronic digital computer. The chief perquisite attached to the prestigious prize is an invitation to address the ACM membership at their yearly convocation. In the past, Turing lectures had often been stimulating fare. Speakers had included some of the most forceful and original thinkers in the field of computing. Outstanding among them were John McCarthy, one of the fathers of artificial intelligence, and Donald Knuth, author of *The Art of Computer Programming,* a comprehensive treatise much admired by software engineers. More often than not, the honorees had welcomed the opportunity to command center stage before an audience of their peers and had offered no-holds-barred critiques of the state of the computer sciences. John Backus would be no exception.

In his opening remarks, he came right to the point: "Programming languages appear to be in trouble." The tone of Backus's lecture was generally gracious and diplomatic, but the overriding message was a sweeping condemnation of contemporary language research. He spoke of a "desperate need for a powerful methodology to help us think about programs" and concluded that "no conventional language even begins to meet that need."

Backus drew a gloomy picture of the headway made in programming during the preceding two decades, suggesting that most new languages did little more than mimic their predecessors. Features added along the way had made languages complicated and increasingly difficult to learn, yet they seemed to offer little in the way of increased productivity. Computer languages had become obese, and the research community that labored year after year to develop new ones, ventured Backus, lacked the intellectual energy to wrestle with difficult or original ideas that might lead to real progress. He argued that a fresh approach was needed.

A different scheme for writing programs—one that was mathematical at heart—had captured his imagination. Somewhat to the bewilderment of his audience, Backus described his latest brainstorm as an approach in which all programs would be made up of functions expressed as simple algebraic formulas. He predicted that the type of language he was trying to perfect would enable programmers to know in advance that their computing solutions would work as planned. In Backus's view, the logic inherent in a mathematical approach to software would not only help programmers write less error-prone code, it would also ease the hardest part of the programmer's job—reasoning through the problems to be solved.

The so-called functional style of programming, which Backus went on to explain to his listeners at the Turing lecture, is just one of several radically different approaches to software development that now compete for the allegiance of programmers. And, though some in the auditorium may have been surprised or even shocked to hear such ideas from the creator of FORTRAN, Backus was not alone in his views.

LANGUAGES SHOWING THEIR AGE
In the years following John Backus's Turing-lecture bombshell, computer programming has passed into a state of creative upheaval. During the late 1970s and

the 1980s, more and more software developers, as they managed information systems for giant corporations or directed small programming shops for hospitals, school systems, or department stores, have concluded that the languages they have been using are no longer sufficient. The conventional dialects are perceived as inadequate because they make the task of programming complex software too difficult and time-consuming. The weaknesses of the old languages are particularly evident when it comes to revising finished software to accommodate additional uses and features. And when programmers look ahead to coming generations of computers that may have more than one central processing unit (CPU) for executing instructions, they see the situation going from bad to worse.

Though no clear solution is on the horizon, a handful of innovators have developed new languages that seem to hold great promise. As might be expected, the new programming dialects bear little resemblance to such workhorse languages as FORTRAN, COBOL, ALGOL, and C. The developers of these new styles of programming have—contrary to Backus's depiction—long since given up picking over the bones of the conventional languages. They are looking for a quantum leap in programming capacity that they have judged to be utterly impossible within the framework of the traditional languages.

In their search, some of the language pioneers have taken their cues from trends in computer hardware. Some, for example, have made parallel processing a starting point for their research. Others begin with the realization that computers linked in far-flung networks, contributing to and drawing from the same banks of data, are different to program than stand-alone systems that do all their own work and speak only to themselves. Still others ignore the hardware and find their inspiration in new organizing principles for software.

The organizational models that are being investigated are quite diverse, for the simple reason that language developers are involved in many different kinds of applications for computers. Some developers of business software, for example, explore an approach in which all sorts of tasks are reduced to problems of database management. This form of programming relies less on sequential, step-by-step instructions to the computer than on flexible, pre-packaged software tools, such as the so-called query languages, which help even very inexperienced computer users to retrieve the information that is available in data files.

Sequencing and ordered strings of commands to the machine are the hallmarks of the traditional style of programming, which is called the imperative approach. A typical element in a program written in an imperative language is a command for the computer to do something, such as set the value of a variable or transfer control to some specified point in the code. At any given moment, the program can be characterized as having an implicit state, which is defined by the value of all the variables and by the current point of control. As the program executes, it may pass through many states. The basic assumption of imperative programming is that the range of possible states in a program is well understood by the software engineer and precisely controlled by the sequence of commands spelled out in the code. Critics of this programming style contend that such an assumption is hopelessly optimistic when software reaches a level of complexity that has become commonplace today.

BREAKING WITH THE VON NEUMANN MODEL

At their core, the traditional imperative programming languages are reflections of the model for computer hardware proposed by John von Neumann in 1945. His description of the basic elements that constitute a computer system has dominated hardware architecture ever since. It includes a memory, a central processing unit—the CPU—to orchestrate operations, and a connection between the two that is capable of sending back and forth, one at a time, units of data, called words. The von Neumann model has been central to the success of the computer industry for more than forty years and is only now subject to serious reconsideration. From the standpoint of the programmer, however, this model poses fundamental problems.

Since any program accomplishes tasks primarily by changing the contents of the computer's memory, the programmer is forced to concentrate on the painstaking task of ushering single words back and forth between the memory and the CPU. This is done by changing the variables written into a program to define the value of individual storage cells in memory. Backus calls this process "word-at-a-time programming" and considers it the root of the unreliability, tardiness, and backbreaking expense that has come to characterize software development.

The procedure is highly detailed and error-prone, because each variable to be changed requires a separate command—called an assignment statement—in the program code. Software written in the standard languages consists mainly of repetitive sequences of assignment statements, broken up occasionally by control instructions that tell when, why, and how many times the assignment statements should be executed. This mode of programming is workable, but it has the undesirable effect of overwhelming programmers with low-level housekeeping chores, often at the expense of the overall organization and efficiency of the software.

The von Neumann origins of the conventional programming languages are also to blame for the difficulties in producing programs that can used over and over again as components of large software systems. Programs written in the traditional languages set up detailed plans assigning each word of data to a particular memory cell and then use other cells to hold additional words describing how to reassemble the data to preserve its meaning. The programs themselves are meaningless except in relation to the detailed storage plan on which they are based. Thus, two programs can only be linked to form a larger program if they have assigned all their data to the same cells and have structured the data identically. In general, this only happens when the programs are jointly planned and written.

During the 1980s, two alternatives to the imperative approach attracted a great deal of attention in the field of language research. One is John Backus's adopted specialty, functional programming, which was raised overnight from years of obscurity by his endorsement in the Turing lecture. This style of programming rejects the von Neumann model and, probably for that reason, has yet to find its way into common application. It is resisted by programmers, in part because it is still in its infancy, but also because it is a radical departure from the familiar ways of producing software. In spite of these liabilities, functional programming has become one of the liveliest areas for ongoing language research. It is viewed by many computer scientists as the best hope for reducing the costs of software development and—perhaps more important—for making full use of the coming generation of parallel-processing computers.

The other alternative to a purely imperative style is called object-oriented programming. This approach is, in some regards, closer to the von Neumann language tradition than is functional programming. For one thing, it preserves the familiar flavor of an ordered sequence of commands to the computer. But object-oriented programming differs in a significant way. It encourages the programmer to use as a model whatever real-world institution the software will be serving. If the programming is for a bank, the software may be modeled on banking operations; if it is for a word processor, it may replicate the functions of a typewriter. Object-oriented programming has already taken practical shape in such languages as Simula, Smalltalk, C++, and Objective C, which are rapidly finding their way into everyday use.

Functional and object-oriented programming work quite differently, but they have certain things in common. For one, they both meet head-on the issue of software reuse. Each in its own way produces independent modules of code that can be linked together with other modules with a minimum of undesirable side effects. Another shared characteristic is that both styles of programming trace their roots to the earliest days of electronic computing. They have taken decades to come into their own.

AN AMALGAM OF FOUNDING PRINCIPLES

The tradition of functional programming began in 1958, when the brilliant mathematician John McCarthy commenced work on a programming language called LISP. Born in Boston and educated at Caltech and Princeton, McCarthy had coined the term "artificial intelligence" in 1955, while employed as an assistant professor of computer science at Dartmouth College, and was a leading figure in a fledgling field of research aimed at creating programs capable of learning and reasoning. By the time he set about developing LISP, he was helping to establish an artificial-intelligence lab at the Massachusetts Institute of Technology. LISP was part of his AI research.

The new language revolved around two borrowed ideas. The first was the notion of list processing, which McCarthy carried over from an earlier AI language known as IPL (for Information Processing Language), developed by Allen Newell and other researchers at the Rand Corporation and later at the Carnegie Institute of Technology. List processing was an attempt to link concepts in the memory of computers in a manner that the artificial-intelligence experts of the time thought might be analogous to the way the human brain stores ideas. In the electronic approach, ideas were the data inside a· computer, represented as lists of symbols and words. The name LISP is an abbreviation of the phrase "list processing."

The other transplanted element of LISP was its distinctive notation, which included three elements: symbols to represent variables and constants, parentheses for grouping the symbols, and the Greek letter λ, or lambda, to represent functions. McCarthy borrowed his notation from the symbols of the lambda calculus, an obscure branch of mathematics introduced in 1931 by a logician named Alonzo Church. The symbols gave McCarthy a means to represent the procedures of his list-processing language in the form of algebraic equations.

These two oddly matched notions—lists and the symbolic expression of ideas as equations—produced an unusual language. With its parentheses inside parentheses inside parentheses, defining lists within lists within lists, the code for LISP looked very strange. And the structure that the language imposed on programmers was also unique for its time. For example, a FORTRAN programmer faced with the task of getting a computer to select items from a list would probably begin by assigning labels to every item. Subsequent instructions in the program would enable it to locate the fifth, tenth, or five-hundredth label, as the situation might require.

The only way a LISP programmer could do the same job would be to have the program count the list from the top each time it needed to find a new item—not a very direct approach. Because McCarthy had invented the language for specific purposes within his research rather than as a general-purpose programming tool, he had not equipped it with an efficient way to assign specific values to variables—the very heart of imperative languages. In spite of this omission, programmers who studied the dialect found it very intriguing. What LISP seemed to do exceedingly well was to help them devise strategies for finding the fifth, tenth, or five-hundredth item on any list, without reference to labels.

The value of LISP in its original form was that it encouraged programmers to look for overall computing solutions, rather than to immediately fixate on the minute details. In fact, that is just about all McCarthy's original version of LISP was good for, since it was impractical on a more detailed level. The more conventional languages had precisely the opposite effect—forcing programmers to plunge right in with decisions about memory assignments and definitions of data structure, and to postpone until later their concerns about overall strategy. In 1960, McCarthy published an influential scientific paper titled "Recursive Functions of Symbolic Expressions," which took a first step toward persuading other computer scientists that LISP was more than just an intriguing experiment.

McCarthy's paper was, for the most part, a description of the mathematical foundations of his new language, but it also provided an interpreter for LISP. An interpreter is similar to a compiler: It is a complex piece of software that converts programs written in a high-level language to the zeros-and-ones "machine code" of a particular computer. Unlike compilers, interpreters do their work a single line at a time, and they have the computer perform each instruction as soon as it becomes comprehensible to the machine. The striking thing about McCarthy's interpreter was that it was written in LISP. McCarthy's point in this seemingly absurd exercise—he was using LISP to explain itself to a computer that did not understand the language—was not lost on his readers. By using his odd-looking symbolic code to give precise descriptions of the workings of an entire language, he proved that LISP was expressive enough to explicate even the most complicated programming tasks. Some programmers were so taken by McCarthy's ingenious program that they used it as a framework for LISP interpreters of their own, written in conventional languages. LISP began to attract a loyal following within the artificial-intelligence community, and a new style of programming was off and running.

Unfortunately, McCarthy's language produced programs that were decidedly sluggish. He had crafted the dialect to please himself as a mathematician and a programmer. In doing so, he had refused to make concessions to the strengths and weaknesses of the von Neumann computer. As a result, computing speed was a problem with LISP right from the beginning. Its programs rarely ran even a tenth as fast as comparable software written in FORTRAN or ALGOL. Nevertheless, the AI programmers who were using LISP took solace in the fact that its code was extremely easy to write and well suited to the business of manipulating lists and creating chains of deduction. They made LISP their language of choice throughout the 1960s.

A LANGUAGE PRONOUNCED "I SWIM"
The first significant contribution to functional programming outside the context of artificial intelligence research was in the work of Peter Landin at Queen Mary College in London during the mid-1960s. Landin was one of a number of computer scientists who were convinced that all programming was unnecessarily complex because it lacked a rigorous mathematical structure. He respected McCarthy's achievement with LISP, but he felt that the language was overly restrictive because of its orientation toward list processing.

Like McCarthy, Landin was influenced by the work of the logician Alonzo Church, and he investigated ways to forge a link between the lambda calculus and high-level programming languages. He concentrated particularly on ALGOL, which was very popular in Europe at that time. Landin was also influenced by another American mathematician named Haskell Curry, a contemporary of Alonzo Church. Curry had formulated another esoteric brand of calculus called combinatory logic, which was based on the premise that any mathematical function, however complicated, could be expressed as a composition of two simple functions.

Landin hoped to fuse the best elements of both these mathematical systems. He wanted languages that would preserve the elegant simplicity with which Church's calculus captured the computational possibilities of functions. And he hoped to add to that structure the flexibility of Curry's procedures for building complex functions from simple ones. In 1966, Landin published a paper describing a family of programming languages that would possess such attributes. He called the languages ISWIM, for "If you See What I Mean." The name

The windows on the computer screen at right are a feature of a multitasking operating system that permits several programs to share the screen while operating side by side within the computer. In this example, based on the OS/2 operating system for desktop computers, a word-processing program occupies the green window. It appears to overlap the blue and yellow windows because it is the program currently accepting input from the keyboard, perhaps as a document is written or revised. The other two windows display the state of other tasks residing in the computer—a section of a large spreadsheet and a database program.

To reach the screen, keystrokes descend through three layers of the operating system, represented as rings in the drawing, to the word-processing program (green), which resides in memory (dark gray) along with the spreadsheet (blue) and database software (yellow). Output from all three is handled by operating-system instructions residing in the innermost ring. These routines maintain the sizes of the windows as specified by the user, position the active window on top of the pile, and ensure that output from each program appears only inside its assigned window.

Glimpses into the Computer

Computers once offered just a single display of their internal proceedings. But as the machines have acquired the ability to juggle multiple tasks, they have also been given the means to create a veritable montage of displays simultaneously on a single computer monitor.

The effect is achieved by dividing the screen into areas called windows, each reserved exclusively for a specific task.

Windows in many word-processing programs, for example, allow at least two documents to occupy the screen simultaneously. Accomplishing this convenience is little trouble for such software because all the windows are under its control. However, to display different programs in windows on the same screen is a more complicated matter. The computer must confine the programs, all of which typically want to take over the entire screen, to their assigned areas.

As shown on these and the following pages, this responsibility, like that of instructing the computer in the fine art of loading multiple programs into memory and coordinating their activities, belongs to the software charged with managing the computer—the operating system.

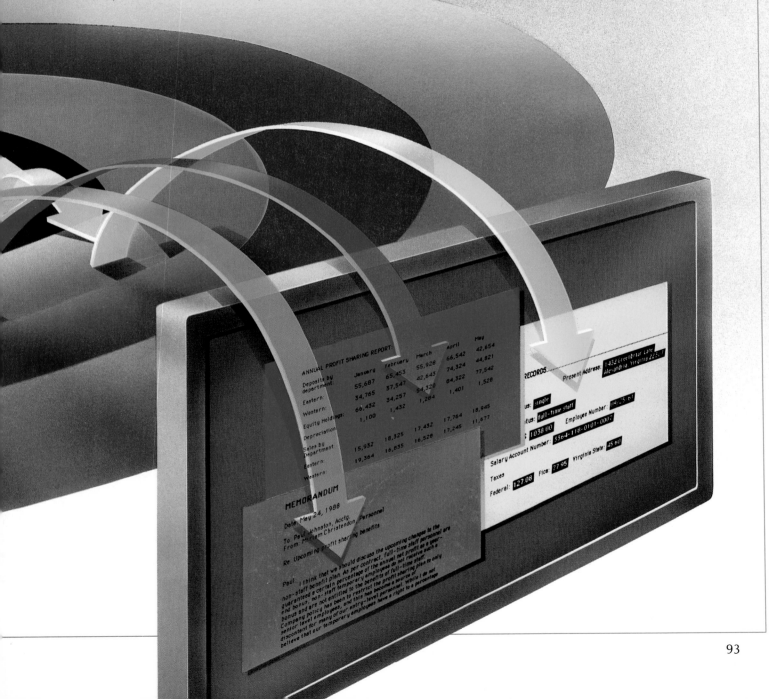

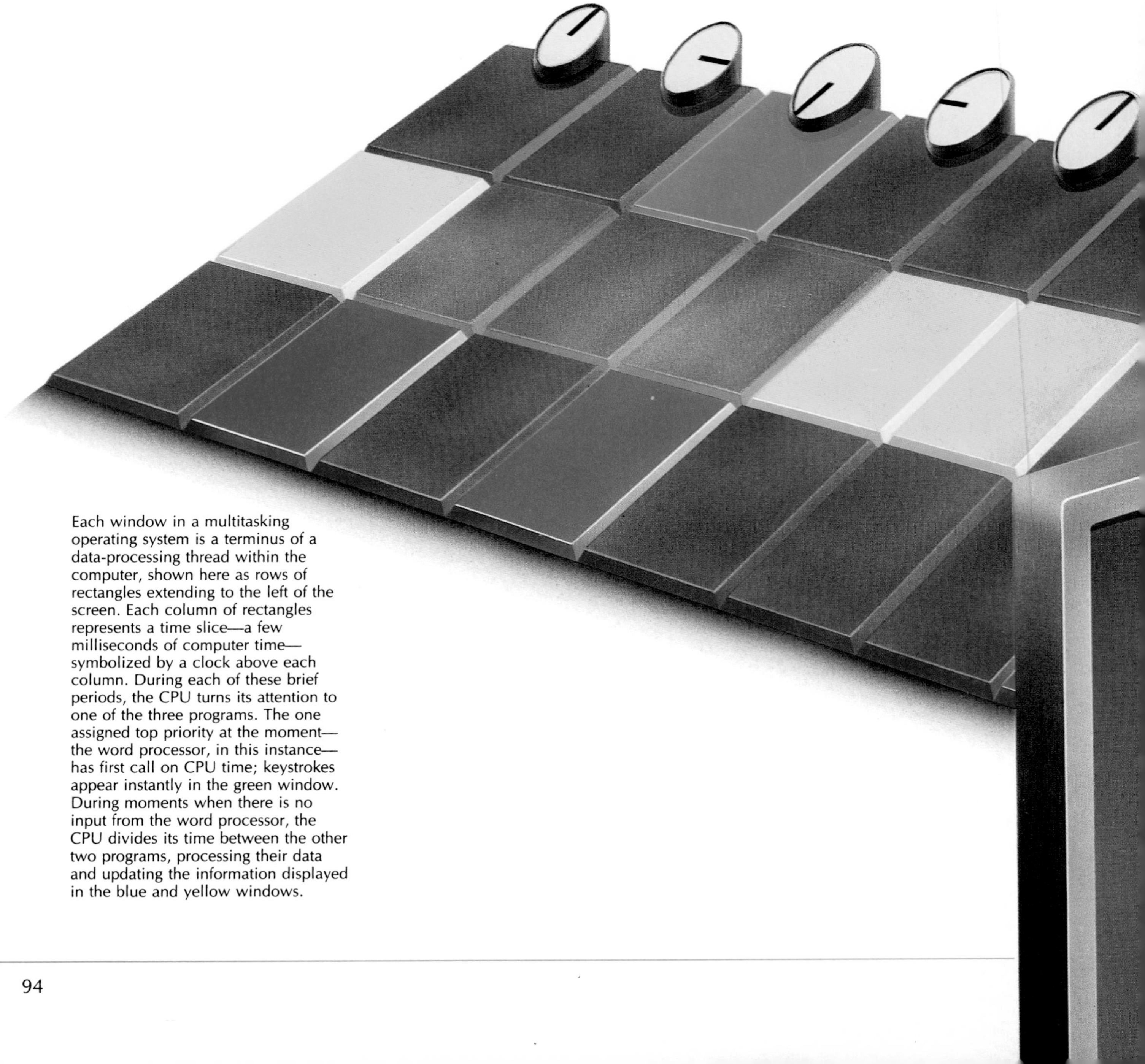

Each window in a multitasking operating system is a terminus of a data-processing thread within the computer, shown here as rows of rectangles extending to the left of the screen. Each column of rectangles represents a time slice—a few milliseconds of computer time—symbolized by a clock above each column. During each of these brief periods, the CPU turns its attention to one of the three programs. The one assigned top priority at the moment—the word processor, in this instance—has first call on CPU time; keystrokes appear instantly in the green window. During moments when there is no input from the word processor, the CPU divides its time between the other two programs, processing their data and updating the information displayed in the blue and yellow windows.

The Ways of Windows

Two kinds of operating systems virtually demand windows for keeping track of goings-on inside the computer. The simpler approach, often called context switching, permits several programs to reside in the computer simultaneously. However, it activates only one of them at a time and updates the contents of that window alone. Data displayed in the other windows is frozen in place, as are the programs behind them. The operating system accomplishes this by restricting each program to part of the computer's memory. Commands issued by the user rapidly switch the attention of the central processing unit (CPU) from one program to another.

A more complicated procedure, called multitasking, permits an operating system to update information displayed in all the windows present on the screen. To do so, the operating system seems almost to run all the programs in memory simultaneously (below). Actually, the CPU is being switched from one to another in accordance with priorities assigned by the programs inside the computer. The software having the highest precedence is usually said to operate in the foreground. Its window is placed on top of the pile, and the CPU processes immediately any commands issued to the program. Progress within programs operating in the background is temporarily suspended. Whenever the foreground program is momentarily idle, the operating system assigns CPU time to the background programs, some of which is used to send information to their windows on the screen.

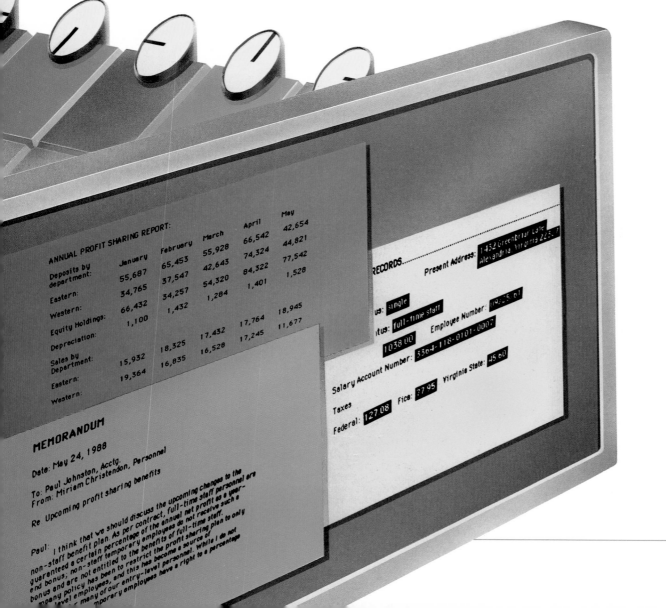

Windows
ad Infinitum

A computer is very likely to have insufficient memory for all the programs and data that a user might wish to load. The result is that software and information already occupying memory space may have to be evicted in order to display additional windows. If handled by the human at the keyboard, this task would be monumentally inconvenient and would rob a window-equipped operating system of its main advantage—to have the widest possible variety of software and data available in the computer. One program and its data would have to be unloaded in favor of another.

An operating system can perform these functions automatically and, in so doing, gives the computer a virtually unlimited capacity for displaying windows. The only additional component necessary is a large-capacity (and preferably speedy) disk drive for storage. As shown on these pages, the operating system, by emptying parts of memory to make room for new tenants, causes memory to appear larger than it actually is. Should old tenants be needed, the operating system reloads them from the disk.

Compaction. Unoccupied memory in a computer, shown here as empty spaces in a stack of bookshelves, is often fragmented *(above)*. For the operating system to determine whether there is enough free space to load a program, memory contents are rearranged so the empty slots form a single block *(above, right)*. The computer then compares the capacity available with the amount of memory required by the program. If there is enough, the program is loaded. In this case, however, the forty-two thousand (42K) bytes of free space is ten thousand bytes smaller than the program to be loaded.

Discarding and swapping. The operating system makes room for a program too large for the memory available by dumping previously loaded material, beginning with the least recently used block of memory. Program code, stored in original form on the disk, is discarded. Data, perhaps altered since it was loaded, is swapped out of memory to the disk. Discarding and swapping continue until enough memory is free for the program.

52K

52K
FREE

Data

Code

bespoke his certainty that a mathematically coherent computer code would be self-explanatory to any competent programmer.

ISWIM did not exactly take the world of programming by storm—in fact, none of the proposed languages were ever fully developed. But Landin's ideas seemed to galvanize a number of like-minded mathematicians, who shared his views on the shortcomings of computer programming. Programming theorists in Europe and the United States, among them the Dutch computer scientist Edsger W. Dijkstra, undertook painstaking analyses of the logical structure of the conventional languages. Their objective was to identify procedures in standard programming that did not lend themselves easily to mathematical description. By showing that these were the primary sources of errors in computer software, they hoped to pave the way for a more orderly approach to programming.

The work was brought to fruition in 1968, when Dijkstra published an article called "Notes on Structured Programming." Dijkstra's central argument in this article was that programming had become a solitary, problem-solving form of activity, based far too heavily on intuition and too little on any sort of disciplined, mathematical process.

Dijkstra's suggested remedy was to produce controlled, logical programs that were less personal and idiosyncratic—software that could be reviewed and improved by a programmer's colleagues. The first step in this direction, Dijkstra

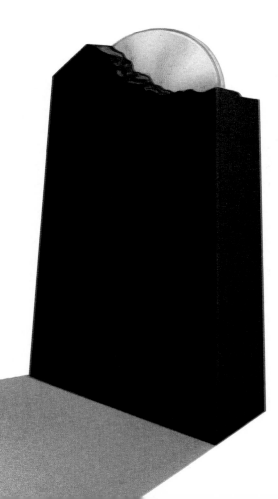

contended, was to eliminate a commonplace programming command known as the unconditional jump, or GOTO statement. Such jumps were convenient in that they allowed the programmer to shift control at any point to any specified line in a program, but they were far too arbitrary and uncontrolled. They defied mathematical description and made computer code extremely difficult to decipher for anyone other than a program's creator.

Although Dijkstra's suggestions were initially greeted with skepticism and alarm, they were eventually borne out by practical experimentation. As a result, some of the most unconstrained programming practices—the GOTO statement being an egregious example—have fallen into general disfavor. Today, structured programming is a fundamental part of most computer-science curricula. In spite of this breakthrough, Peter Landin and the other advocates of functional programming, who were at least partially responsible for the rise of structured techniques, continued to labor in obscurity.

A COMING-OUT FOR FUNCTIONAL PROGRAMMING

John Backus changed all that in his Turing lecture by lauding the efforts of the functional programmers and suggesting that the conventional languages—including his own brainchild, FORTRAN—could not be adapted to the new approach. On the strength of his recommendation, interest in function-based programming intensified overnight, and within a few years new languages had begun to proliferate. A potpourri of functional dialects appeared, mostly in computer-science departments at universities in the United Kingdom, the United States, and the Scandinavian nations. They were identified by obscure code names, such as Miranda and Hope, or by acronyms, such as ML, SASL, VAL, and ALFL. Most of them shared common elements of syntax, so that they were fairly easily understood from one to the next. The growth was so rapid, however, that within ten years of Backus's lecture, computer scientists working in the field of functional programming were concerned that the lack of a standard might hamper the eventual acceptance of their approach. In September 1987, an international panel convened in Portland, Oregon, to lay the groundwork for a unified language called Haskell (after Haskell Curry). The dialect was completed in December 1988.

Characteristically, the brand of functional programming that the independent-minded Backus has pursued since 1977 has a flavor all its own. He rejected the framework of the lambda calculus, which has been a dominant feature of most other functional languages. Backus feels that Church's system, which describes all of the computational possibilities of mathematical functions, gives too many options to programmers and thus opens the way for chaotically unpredictable software—the equivalent of using GOTO statements in the conventional languages. His alternative has taken shape in a dialect called FL (for Functional Level programming language), which Backus introduced in 1986 and continues to refine with the help of other language experts at the IBM Almaden Research Center in San Jose, California.

BUILDING NEW PROGRAMS FROM OLD ONES

One of the most important features of FL is its emphasis on software reuse. It provides an approach in which existing programs can be melded together by means of a limited set of so-called program-forming operations to create new programs, which can in turn be used to build even larger systems. The existing programs are nothing more than combinations of mathematical functions and thus are universally applicable. For example, simple functions of addition and division are combined in the program "average (a, b) = half $(a + b)$," which transforms any pair of numbers, a and b, to their average value. Because such a program holds true no matter what the value of a and b, it can be used over and over again regardless of the specifics of the data involved in a particular software problem.

The program-forming operations are the key to FL because they assist programmers in formulating strategies for their computing solutions and allow them to express their plans very succinctly as combinations of programs, without worrying about too many details. For example, the program for finding averages can be written in FL as "average = half ∘ +." The program-forming operation represented by the tiny circle (∘) is called "composition." Using this operation, two simple programs, "half" and "+," are combined to build the program "average," with the composition symbol instructing the computer to execute the procedure to its right (+) first, then apply the procedure on its left to the result. Composition is one of half a dozen similar techniques—some of them borrowed from Haskell Curry's combinatory logic—used to build up new FL programs from existing ones.

Another common program-forming operation called "construction," which is symbolized by a pair of square brackets, illustrates the advantage of a language like FL for programming parallel-processing computers. When two programs are combined by construction, they are applied to the same number and yield a pair of results. For example, the construction "[square, double]" applied to 4 yields 16 and 8—the square of 4 and its value multiplied by 2. When programs are linked in this way, it does not matter which of them is executed first, because the same pair of values will result in either case. Thus, the programmer writing code in FL can readily identify jobs that can be assigned to different CPUs for simultaneous processing.

Another advantage of Backus's program-forming operations is that they possess certain mathematical properties that can help programmers find the most efficient computing solutions. For example, a programmer who has brought together three existing programs called F, G, and H to form the more complicated program "$[F ∘ H, G ∘ H]$" can use simple algebra to deduce that precisely the same results can be had from the mathematically equivalent "$[F, G] ∘ H$." The latter solution is more efficient because it only requires that program H be run once, rather than twice.

John Backus and the other functional pioneers believe that the adoption of their languages will take a bigger bite out of the cost of producing software than FORTRAN did when it ushered out the era of programming in machine code. Several issues remain to be resolved, however, before the new languages can be commercially viable.

The biggest problem is still one of speed. Because the functional languages are not specifically geared to the von Neumann model of computing, their programs do not run as fast as programs written in the conventional languages. Although improvements in the most recently developed functional languages have narrowed this gap significantly, many computer scientists are openly skeptical that equivalent speeds can ever be achieved.

One of two things will have to happen for the functional languages to make their mark. Either the languages will have to be substantially improved or there will have to be a fundamental change in hardware architecture that allows them to run more efficiently. Oddly enough, the upsurge of research in non-von Neumann architectures during the 1980s—some of it specifically carried out with functional programming in mind—makes the second possibility appear the more likely of the two.

LANGUAGES THAT DEFINE OBJECTS

While functional programming awaits further refinement and the arrival of more compatible hardware, the object-oriented style of computing has stepped in to fill the breach for workaday programmers of the traditional languages. This approach is in its own way as fresh and original as the inventions of McCarthy, Landin, and Backus.

Object-oriented programming is based on the notion that the subject matter of a program should have a direct and explicit representation in the software. For example, a program that will simulate electronic circuits should contain some easy and obvious means of representing transistors, wires, switches, resistors, and the like.

Since 1981, when this programming method first grabbed the attention of the software community, at least a dozen languages that revolve around the concept of objects have come into use. An object is the basic unit or module of code in this approach. Each one consists of a set of program instructions and a discrete portion of data that the software will manipulate.

An illustration of the concept is seen in the popular Macintosh personal computer made by Apple Computer Company of Cupertino, California. When a Macintosh user requests a text file—be it an interoffice memo, a personal letter, or the manuscript for a magazine article—the computer supplies both the data for that piece of writing and the word-processing software so that the contents of the file can be changed or appended. On many other systems, the same process takes two separate steps—loading the word processor and calling up the text file.

The breakthrough for object-oriented programming was the introduction of a commercial version of the language Smalltalk in 1981. The California-based researchers who had been refining this language throughout the 1970s were

101

the first to use the term "object-oriented." However, the concept of objects goes back—far back—to the work of two inventive Norwegians, Kristen Nygaard and Ole-Johan Dahl.

A NORWEGIAN LANGUAGE FOR SIMULATIONS

In 1948, the twenty-two-year-old Nygaard, fresh from his university training in mathematics, accepted a post at the Norwegian Defense Research Establishment (NDRE) in Oslo. He had not joined the NDRE entirely by choice—he was fulfilling an obligatory term of military service—but he wound up staying at the research center for more than eleven years. He was initially assigned to work as an assistant to Jan Vaumund Garwick, a versatile scientist who, in addition to other accomplishments, played a significant role in promoting the computer sciences in Norway by steering talented young researchers into the field. Nygaard's earliest work, however, depended not at all on computers, which were still quite rare in his country. He helped Garwick with the development of plans for Norway's first nuclear reactor. By 1950, Nygaard had produced by hand a mathematical model that simulated the functions of the proposed system. The specific purpose of the model was to enable engineers to calculate the optimum diameter of the uranium rods in the reactor's core, and the work was successful in that regard.

Nygaard's simulation relied on a procedure called the Monte Carlo method, which yields approximate solutions to complicated problems by a process of sampling random numbers. Monte Carlo techniques had led to many important discoveries in the field of nuclear physics, but the procedure was laborious to do by hand, and in the years following World War II, the Monte Carlo method had been successfully programmed on the computers at the Los Alamos Laboratory in New Mexico.

Since Nygaard's arrival at the NDRE, he and Garwick had followed with interest developments abroad in the production of electronic computers. They were joined in 1952 by another draftee, Ole-Johan Dahl, who shared their enthusiasm for the new machines. Between 1951 and 1953, the NDRE team developed their own computer—a homemade electromechanical job built around an old-fashioned punch-card calculator. A year later, the NDRE decided to invest in a more substantial hardware system—a British-made Mercury computer from Ferranti Ltd. in Manchester.

In the process of developing basic software for the new machine, Garwick and Dahl began studying the principles of computer-language design. For his part, Nygaard remained focused on expanding the role of simulations in the design of everything from airports to weapons systems. Gradually, the Mercury computer came to play a central role in his computations, and through hard experience Nygaard learned that the few well-developed programming languages that existed at that time were not particularly well-suited to the job of producing simulations.

In May 1960, Kristen Nygaard left the NDRE to build up the Norwegian Computing Center (NCC), a government-sponsored research institute devoted to encouraging the use of computers in the fields of operational research, numerical analysis, and applied statistics. Many of the projects he undertook at the NCC revolved around simulations, and he still lacked the tools to do the job efficiently. Since he was his own boss now, he set about developing a more appropriate programming language. By January 1962, the project had acquired the name Simula.

It quickly became evident to Nygaard that he was long on experience in developing simulations and short on expertise in the theories of language design. He began a correspondence with Ole-Johan Dahl and, in March of 1963, he persuaded his former colleague to join the staff of the NCC. Between that spring and the end of 1964, the two scientists completed a design for Simula as both a written system for describing physical systems and a simulation programming language.

By all accounts, the collaboration was a stormy one, marked by frequent shouting matches. On one occasion, a particularly noisy debate convinced a newcomer to the NCC that Nygaard and Dahl were on the verge of coming to blows. They never did, however, and in retrospect both men feel that their explosive working style made Simula a better language. Every new idea was challenged and had to be proved to the satisfaction of both parties.

In 1965, the NCC introduced the first commercial version of Simula, complete with a compiler to run on the UNIVAC 1107 computer. The language revolved around elements called processes, which were precursors to the objects in today's languages. Programs in Simula were structured as systems of interrelated components (processes), defined by what they could do and controlled by messages that coordinated their prescribed functions. The language was highly specialized—custom-tailored to the task of creating simulations. But as Nygaard began spreading word of the language by teaching it to programmers who had been trained in FORTRAN and ALGOL, he found that there was a great deal of interest in applying his ideas to other applications that had nothing to do with simulation. He and Dahl began exploring the possibility of rewriting Simula as a general-purpose programming language.

In September 1965, the two Norwegians resumed their pitched battles in an effort to work such a change. They emerged a little more than two years later with an expanded version of Simula, which they named Simula 67. Several more years passed before compilers were in place to support any actual programming. The first compilers were introduced in the spring of 1969 for Control Data 3000 and 6000 computers. IBM followed suit in May 1972, with compilers for the System/360 and 370 machines. Even with compilers available, however, use of the language was slow in building, and Simula remained a little-known dialect until more popular languages appeared that borrowed its unique approach. Kristen Nygaard believes that the initially lukewarm reception of Simula 67 can be attributed to its origins in a tiny institute in a small country, off the beaten track for innovations in computer technology.

Almost from the start, however, the dialect that Nygaard created with Dahl exerted a strong influence on language researchers. All the essential elements of today's object-oriented languages were operational in Simula 67. Independent modules of code called objects, with self-contained data and narrowly defined sets of operations, interacted with one another by sending messages requesting action or passing along information. Similar objects were organized hierarchically in classes *(page 74)*, so that the structure of any Simula program was readily obvious to any programmer reading the code. Also characteristic of the derivative languages to follow, new objects in Simula 67 were created by a process of duplication called inheritance. Object-oriented programming was ready and waiting for the software industry to awaken to the need for change.

PROGRAMMING AS CHILD'S PLAY

The language Smalltalk, which mixed the Simula approach with some imaginative techniques for interacting with computers by means of graphic symbols, was the magnet that first attracted general notice to the ideas of Nygaard and Dahl. Lending credence to Nygaard's assertion that Simula was ignored because of its obscure origins, Smalltalk was born in one of the recognized hotbeds of computer innovation—at the Xerox Palo Alto Research Center (PARC) in the heart of Silicon Valley. PARC was well known for its creative staff; people expected PARC to be the source of important ideas. The moving force behind Smalltalk was Alan Kay, a peripatetic intellectual who is widely regarded as one of the genuine visionaries of California computer research. Years later, Kay's graphical interface for Smalltalk would be the model for the approach adopted in the Macintosh personal computer. For all his inventiveness, however, Kay is quick to acknowledge his debt to Nygaard and Dahl for the central ideas of Smalltalk.

The original Smalltalk development was part of a larger scheme that Kay had been pondering since his graduate student days at the University of Utah. He brought with him to PARC in 1971 a highly original plan for a personal computer that was intended as a learning tool for children. Called Dynabook, his proposed system would be no bigger than a school notebook, yet it would have sophisticated text and graphics capabilities, and it would be able to communicate with every database and library in the world. Kay worked from the assumption that the language for this system would have to be simple enough for any curious child to master.

Needless to say, Kay's vision was ahead of its time. In 1971, there were no personal computers, much less sophisticated ones. By 1973, however, Xerox PARC engineers had developed a working computer, called the Alto, that incorporated some of Kay's ideas. Based on one of the first microprocessors, the Alto could manipulate complicated text and pictures. Almost the size of a dishwasher, it was no book, but it was small enough to fit under a desk. But the most impressive thing about the Alto was the language that made it run. Kay's maiden version of Smalltalk, written in 1972, could partition the Alto's high-resolution screen into multiple windows, simultaneously presenting data from several different files in computer memory. And with its clever use of objects, classes, and inheritance, it was impressively easy to use—though perhaps not simple enough for third graders.

Between 1973 and 1980, the Smalltalk team at PARC—at first with Kay's assistance and later without him, after he left to pursue the goals of Dynabook with the Atari Corporation—produced four increasingly refined versions of the language. The development process culminated with Smalltalk 80, which was licensed for use at universities and research centers. Interest in the language spread quickly, and by 1986 Smalltalk was a marketable commodity finding its way into commercial applications. Smalltalk has been used for everything from programming work stations for petroleum engineers to helping airline analysts compute the most profitable fare structures.

MICROCOMPUTER HOUSES JUMP ON BOARD

The success of Smalltalk 80 pumped life into the object-oriented approach and inspired a flock of other Simula imitators. Among the most prominent of the new languages are C++ and Objective C (both of which are adaptations of the popular dialect C), Object Pascal, and a derivative of LISP called CLOS (for Common LISP Object System). What these languages all have in common

is an efficient programming style that relies on a process of refinement: The programmer creates new code by making minor modifications in programs that already exist.

Applications developed in this way are built up in stages, with the programmer creating a partial solution, testing it, adding features, testing again, and so on until a system is complete. In addition to producing software that is easy to maintain because it is understandable to outside programmers, these languages provide a useful basis for computer-aided software engineering (CASE).

The personal computer industry has been especially quick to embrace this trend in programming. William Gates, chairman of the most successful of the microcomputer programming houses, Microsoft Corporation, has made the object-oriented approach an important part of his company's software development scheme. Apple Computer founder Steven Jobs—who left the company in a power struggle in 1985 and launched a new venture called NeXT—in 1988 announced a powerful personal computer whose built-in software includes object-oriented programming tools that make the machine exceptionally easy to program.

It has taken nearly forty years, but the seeds of fundamental change in programming, planted by language designers such as Nygaard, Dahl, McCarthy, and Backus, seem at last to have taken hold. Only time will tell whether the object-oriented style or its functional counterpart will dominate the software industry. Perhaps neither will: Some other wholly different approach to programming could emerge and usher them both back to obscurity. The other unpredictable factor in the long-term equation is whether the hardware industry will go on perpetuating the von Neumann model—producing ever-faster, more powerful machines, without heed to the troubles of the programmers trying to make use of all that speed and power. Alternatively, hardware designers may be forced to develop new designs that smooth the job of producing software. Either way, computer programming must find its way to a more efficient future.

A Program for Parallelism

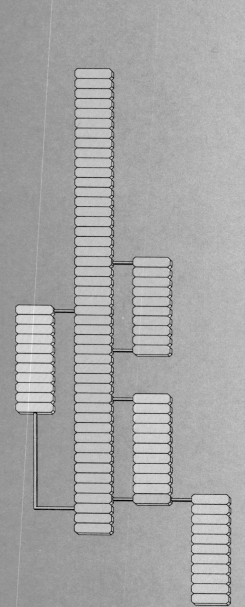

In the perpetual quest for greater speed, computer designers are finding ways to build machines capable of performing dozens, hundreds, even thousands of operations simultaneously—a strategy known as parallel processing. By putting multiple processors to work on a single problem, parallel systems offer unprecedented time savings in the execution of programs, the most complex of which can run to millions of lines of coding.

Designing the hardware and circuitry for such systems is a challenge in itself, but developing appropriate software is an even more daunting prospect. Most tried-and-true programs, called "dusty decks" after the stacks of punch cards once used to load programs into computers, follow step-by-step procedures ideally suited to traditional sequential computers, which execute just one operation at a time. To avoid the inevitable slowdown of processing instructions one after another in turn, some researchers are experimenting with entirely new program-writing methods specifically geared to parallel hardware; existing programs, however, would have to be completely rewritten.

An alternative path to parallelism would preserve the colossal investment of time and money in current software. Special programs, called parallelizing compilers, search the text of sequential programs for operations that can in fact be done in parallel, even though the program is not written in a special format . The compilers then rearrange instructions for simultaneous execution on multiple processing units.

One type of parallelizing compiler is illustrated on the following pages. It extracts parallelism from sequential code by packing several simple instructions, such as "add these two numbers" or "load this value from memory," into what is termed a very long instruction word (VLIW). Instead of the 32-bit instruction typically used by most computers, a very long instruction word may be up to 1,024 bits long, allowing multiple operations to be carried out at the same instant. In this way, VLIW software turns the one-lane instruction path of an ordinary computer into a multilane expressway.

The Functional Basics

Computers and programmers rarely speak the same language. Most programs are written in high-level languages, such as FORTRAN or C, that free the programmer from having to think about the many specific steps involved in performing even the simplest processing tasks. The computer, however, can understand only the digital language of binary code—the streams of zeros and ones that actually control the switches of its circuitry. To bridge the gap, a compiler program first translates high-level statements into the more detailed instructions required by the computer, generating a sequence of commands such as that shown below, at left; these commands will, in turn, be transformed into binary code.

C = A + B

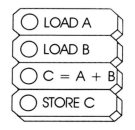

A four-step process. A single program statement, $C = A + B$, in a high-level language *(top)* must be translated by a compiler into more basic instructions *(above)* that tell the computer exactly what to do: Bring two values, A and B, from memory into the processing unit, perform the actual calculation, then store the result.

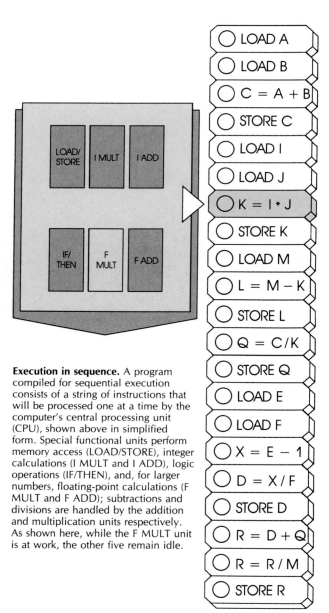

Execution in sequence. A program compiled for sequential execution consists of a string of instructions that will be processed one at a time by the computer's central processing unit (CPU), shown above in simplified form. Special functional units perform memory access (LOAD/STORE), integer calculations (I MULT and I ADD), logic operations (IF/THEN), and, for larger numbers, floating-point calculations (F MULT and F ADD); subtractions and divisions are handled by the addition and multiplication units respectively. As shown here, while the F MULT unit is at work, the other five remain idle.

In translating programs, compilers must take into account variations in the architecture, or internal organization, of different types of computers. Compilers thus play a crucial role in adapting software to take full advantage of processing shortcuts built into the hardware. For example, many advanced computers have specialized features that allow the next instruction to be fetched from memory while the preceding one is being executed; a compiling program controls this overlapping of tasks, in some cases doubling the computer's processing speed.

Another technique relies on the creation of specialized circuitry, called functional units, that are custom-designed to perform the most common operations in the shortest possible time. A sequential computer extracts minimal benefits from such an arrangement; although each functional unit will execute its designated task faster than a general-purpose processor, each unit must still wait in turn to be fed an instruction, with the result that only one unit at a time can be active. But functional units set the stage for parallelism; as illustrated below, a parallelizing compiler can keep several functional units busy at once by grouping operations into very long instruction words, each with space for as many individual commands as there are functional units wired into the computer's processor.

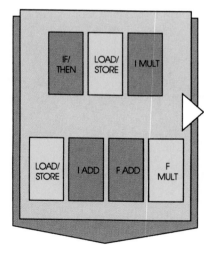

Putting more units to work. A parallelizing compiler takes the same program used by a sequential computer and rearranges it into very long instruction words, represented by the seven rows at right. Each of the seven columns matches a different functional unit in the CPU. The highlighted word contains two memory requests, LOAD E and LOAD M, and an arithmetic calculation, $K = I * J$, which are executed simultaneously by the two LOAD/STORE units and the F MULT unit. In this way, the CPU can perform up to seven operations in parallel.

Rules for Restructuring

As a VLIW compiler searches for operations that can be carried out in parallel, it must obey certain rules designed to keep the program running without a hitch. For example, instructions can be executed together only if the required functional units are simultaneously available. Since there are only two LOAD/STORE units in the simplified CPU on the previous page, the compiler can combine no more than two LOAD or STORE instructions in the same instruction word.

The compiler also must not schedule an arithmetic operation, such as addition, before the two values to be added have been loaded from memory. The concept underlying this rule, called data precedence, means that some functional units may have to remain idle while waiting for data from memory or for the result of another calculation. Consequently, instruction words can include blank sections that prevent the computer from operating at maximum efficiency.

A further complication is introduced by decision-making instructions, called conditional branch statements, that may cause the program to proceed in a new direction. The conditional branch statement highlighted at right tells the computer to "jump" to a new instruction path if the value L is less than or equal to zero. Because it does not know precisely where the program is headed, the compiler apparently must schedule the conditional statement before any computations that follow it, a situation that gives rise to even more instruction-word blanks. However, studies of real-world programs indicate that programs typically branch the same way up to 95 percent of the time. Using statistics derived from testing real programs, the VLIW compiler can thus determine the most likely path a program will follow—called the main trace—and then schedule operations based on this assumption, filling in as many blanks as possible, as soon as possible. The trick to the strategy is anticipating and compensating for errors that may occur when the program occasionally veers off the main trace (pages 113-114).

As shown at right, the twenty-eight sequential instructions of this program have been reshuffled and compressed into just seven VLIW instructions, in essence speeding up execution by a factor of four.

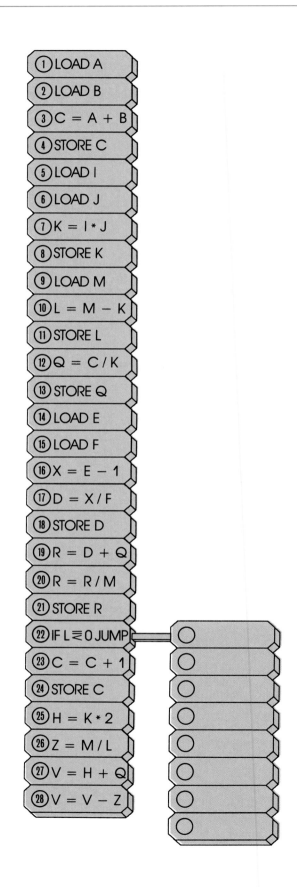

1. LOAD A
2. LOAD B
3. C = A + B
4. STORE C
5. LOAD I
6. LOAD J
7. K = I * J
8. STORE K
9. LOAD M
10. L = M − K
11. STORE L
12. Q = C / K
13. STORE Q
14. LOAD E
15. LOAD F
16. X = E − 1
17. D = X / F
18. STORE D
19. R = D + Q
20. R = R / M
21. STORE R
22. IF L ≦ 0 JUMP
23. C = C + 1
24. STORE C
25. H = K * 2
26. Z = M / L
27. V = H + Q
28. V = V − Z

The first two operations, LOAD A and LOAD B, can be carried out simultaneously by the two memory access functional units and are thus compiled into the same VLIW instruction.

In the second instruction word, two more values, *I* and *J*, are loaded from memory. The addition $C = A + B$, which had to wait for *A* and *B* to be loaded, can now be performed.

The values *E* and *M* are loaded, and the multiplication $K = I * J$ is carried out. The initial instruction words are dominated by LOAD operations that provide data for calculations in the other functional units. The LOAD E step has been advanced from Step 14 in the sequential program.

This instruction word employs six of the seven functional units in parallel. The value of *C* computed two cycles earlier is now copied to main memory using the instruction STORE C. One other memory function is performed, and four arithmetic functions are carried out on previously loaded data.

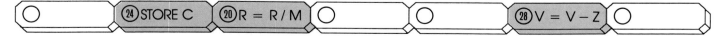

A new value for *C* is computed in this step, but because it has not yet been stored, main memory still holds the original value. Two more calculations are performed, and the values *K* and *L* are copied to main memory.

| ㉒IF L ≦ 0 JUMP | ⑬ STORE Q | ○ | ⑱ STORE D | ⑲R = D + Q | ㉗V = Q + H | ○ |

The conditional branch statement, Step 22 in the sequential program, is now executed, along with two computations and two stores. Depending on the value of *L*, the conditional statement will either keep the program on the main trace or cause it to jump to a subsidiary one.

| ○ | ㉔ STORE C | ⑳R = R / M | ○ | ○ | ㉘V = V − Z | ○ |

The instruction STORE C copies the new value of *C*, computed two steps earlier, to main memory. The division operation $R = R / M$, which preceded the conditional branch in the sequential listing, now comes after it because the appropriate functional unit was previously occupied on the original calculation of *R*.

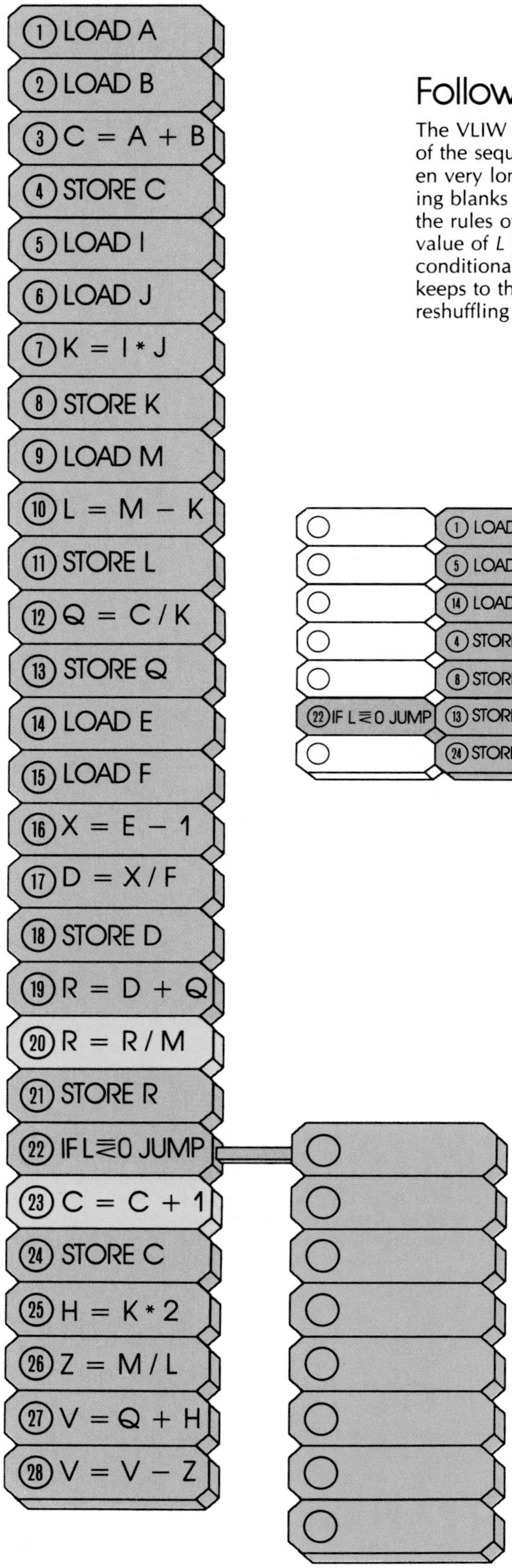

① LOAD A
② LOAD B
③ C = A + B
④ STORE C
⑤ LOAD I
⑥ LOAD J
⑦ K = I * J
⑧ STORE K
⑨ LOAD M
⑩ L = M − K
⑪ STORE L
⑫ Q = C / K
⑬ STORE Q
⑭ LOAD E
⑮ LOAD F
⑯ X = E − 1
⑰ D = X / F
⑱ STORE D
⑲ R = D + Q
⑳ R = R / M
㉑ STORE R
㉒ IF L ≦ 0 JUMP
㉓ C = C + 1
㉔ STORE C
㉕ H = K * 2
㉖ Z = M / L
㉗ V = Q + H
㉘ V = V − Z

Following the Main Trace

The VLIW compiler compacts the main trace of the sequential program into a block of seven very long instruction words *(below)*, keeping blanks to a minimum without breaking the rules of data precedence. So long as the value of L is greater than zero and the conditional jump is not invoked, the program keeps to the main trace and the compiler's reshuffling of operations poses no problems.

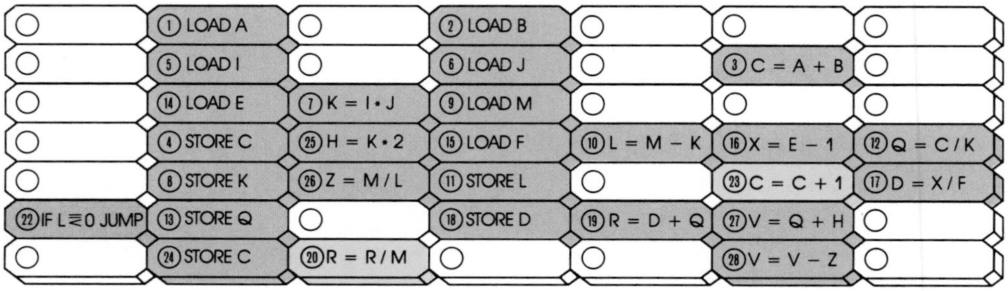

○	① LOAD A	○	② LOAD B	○	○	○
○	⑤ LOAD I	○	⑥ LOAD J	○	③ C = A + B	○
○	⑭ LOAD E	⑦ K = I * J	⑨ LOAD M	○	○	○
○	④ STORE C	㉕ H = K * 2	⑮ LOAD F	⑩ L = M − K	⑯ X = E − 1	⑫ Q = C / K
○	⑧ STORE K	㉖ Z = M / L	⑪ STORE L	○	㉓ C = C + 1	⑰ D = X / F
㉒ IF L ≦ 0 JUMP	⑬ STORE Q	○	⑱ STORE D	⑲ R = D + Q	㉗ V = Q + H	○
○	㉔ STORE C	⑳ R = R / M	○	○	㉘ V = V − Z	○

As part of the reorganizing of instructions, statement No. 23, $C = C + 1$, which follows the conditional branch in the sequential code, has been moved ahead in the VLIW code to an instruction word that precedes the branch. This allows the operation to be performed by a functional unit that would otherwise be idle. The opposite situation, an overbooked functional unit, causes No. 20, $R = R / M$, to be moved from its position before the branch to one following. Relocating these operations relative to the conditional branch raises the possibility of errors should the jump instruction be invoked and the program leave the main trace.

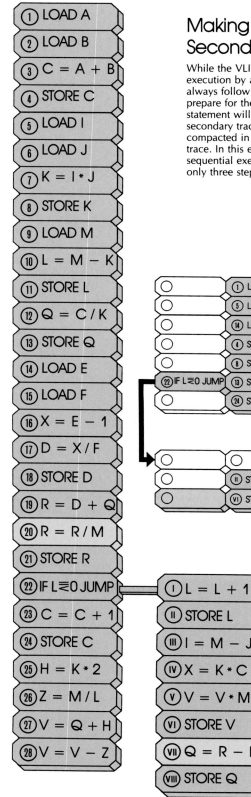

Making the Jump to a Secondary Path

While the VLIW compiler can speed execution by assuming that the program will always follow the main trace, it must also prepare for the possibility that a branch statement will lead to an alternate path. This secondary trace *(below, blue)* is then compacted in the same way as the main trace. In this example, the eight steps of a sequential execution have been reduced to only three steps of parallel computation.

Main trace:

| 1 LOAD A |
| 2 LOAD B |
| 3 C = A + B |
| 4 STORE C |
| 5 LOAD I |
| 6 LOAD J |
| 7 K = I * J |
| 8 STORE K |
| 9 LOAD M |
| 10 L = M − K |
| 11 STORE L |
| 12 Q = C / K |
| 13 STORE Q |
| 14 LOAD E |
| 15 LOAD F |
| 16 X = E − 1 |
| 17 D = X / F |
| 18 STORE D |
| 19 R = D + Q |
| 20 R = R / M |
| 21 STORE R |
| 22 IF L ≦ 0 JUMP |
| 23 C = C + 1 |
| 24 STORE C |
| 25 H = K * 2 |
| 26 Z = M / L |
| 27 V = Q + H |
| 28 V = V − Z |

Secondary path:

| I L = L + 1 |
| II STORE L |
| III I = M − J |
| IV X = K * C |
| V V = V * M |
| VI STORE V |
| VII Q = R − I |
| VIII STORE Q |

Compacted main trace:

	① LOAD A		② LOAD B			
	⑤ LOAD I		⑥ LOAD J		③ C = A + B	
	⑭ LOAD E	⑦ K = I * J	⑨ LOAD M			
	④ STORE C	㉕ H = K * 2	⑮ LOAD F	⑩ L = M − K	⑯ X = E − 1	⑫ Q = C / K
	⑧ STORE K	㉖ Z = M / L	⑪ STORE L		㉓ C = C + 1	⑰ D = X / F
㉒ IF L ≦ 0 JUMP	⑬ STORE Q		⑱ STORE D		⑲ R = D + Q	㉗ V = Q + H
	㉔ STORE C	⑳ R = R / M			㉘ V = V − Z	

Compacted secondary trace:

				Ⅰ L = L + 1		
	Ⅱ STORE L	Ⅳ X = K * C		Ⅲ I = M − J	Ⅶ Q = R − I	Ⅴ V = X * M
	Ⅵ STORE V		Ⅷ STORE Q			

The shuffling of the original sequence of instructions leads to an error in the secondary trace at No. VII, the subtraction operation $Q = R − I$. To obtain a correct answer, this instruction needs the value of R calculated in statement No. 20, $R = R / M$. But because No. 20 is now in an instruction word that follows the conditional branch in the main trace, the program shifts to the secondary trace before the computation is performed. If the compiler stopped its work at this point, an incorrect value for R would be used in No. VII, making the value of Q and any other dependent calculations incorrect.

Steps to Ensure an Accurate Run

In the same way that the compiler follows rules for the initial reshuffling of sequential operations, it must also obey certain guidelines as it establishes main and subsidiary traces. When it comes to a branch statement, the compiler performs a series of boundary tests *(page 9)*, carefully analyzing its scheduling of operations relative to the branch. It looks for two main types of errors: operations that should not have been performed before the conditional branch, and operations that should have been performed before the branch but were not. The diagrams on these pages illustrate two typical strategies a compiler would employ to prevent these potential errors from waylaying the run of a program.

To deal with operations that were moved ahead of the branch, the compiler can simply wait until after the branch to store the result; if the program leaves the main trace, the interim result is, in effect, ignored, and the previously stored value is used in the secondary trace, as was originally intended. Conversely, when a necessary operation is delayed until after the branch, the compiler merely copies it into the secondary trace. The duplicate instruction, known as compensation code, ensures that the operation is performed no matter which path the program follows.

Compensation code does increase the overall number of instructions in the program, but there is rarely any additional cost in execution time. In most cases, this new code, compacted into instruction words along with the program's original instructions, is processed by functional units that would otherwise have had nothing to do.

① LOAD A
② LOAD B
③ $C = A + B$
④ STORE C
⑤ LOAD I
⑥ LOAD J
⑦ $K = I * J$
⑧ STORE K
⑨ LOAD M
⑩ $L = M - K$
⑪ STORE L
⑫ $Q = C / K$
⑬ STORE Q
⑭ LOAD E
⑮ LOAD F
⑯ $X = E - 1$
⑰ $D = X / F$
⑱ STORE D
⑲ $R = D + Q$
⑳ $R = R / M$
㉑ STORE R
㉒ IF $L \leqq 0$ JUMP
㉓ $C = C + 1$
㉔ STORE C
㉕ $H = K * 2$
㉖ $Z = M / L$
㉗ $V = Q + H$
㉘ $V = V - Z$

Ⅰ $L = L + 1$
Ⅱ STORE L
Ⅲ $I = M - J$
Ⅳ $X = K * C$
Ⅴ $V = V * M$
Ⅵ STORE V
Ⅶ $Q = R - I$
Ⅷ STORE Q

Delaying a store. Because of the way in which the original sequential program *(left)* is arranged, the instruction $X = K * C$, No. IV in the secondary path, is intended to use the value of C calculated in step No. 3, $C = A + B$. But in the VLIW code *(opposite)*, the compiler has scheduled No. 23, $C = C + 1$, ahead of the conditional branch, altering the value of C. The compiler avoids an error in this case by delaying No. 24, STORE C, until after the branch. Should the program jump to the secondary trace, the old value of C will be used, ensuring accurate calculations.

Duplicating a command. Since step No. 20, $R = R / M$, has been rescheduled after the conditional branch in the main trace *(below)*, the compiler must copy it into the secondary trace *(bottom)*. Thus, no matter which path is followed, the correct sequence of operations is carried out; the updated value of R is available at step No. VII, and $Q = R - I$ gives a correct result. Although an extra instruction has been added, it will be executed in parallel during the first instruction word, so it has no effect on how fast the program runs.

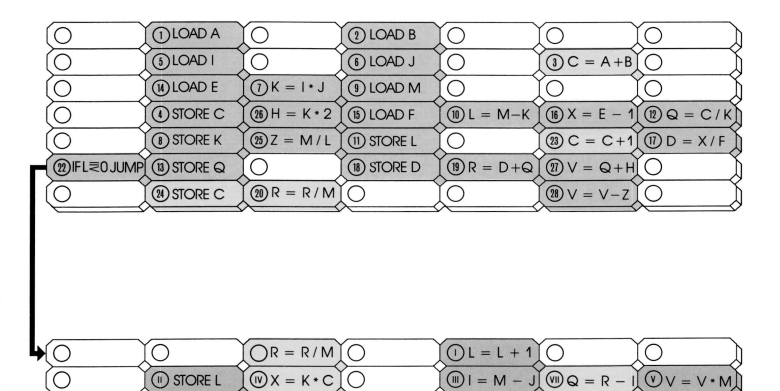

Scheduling Multiple Pathways

The benefits of making an educated guess about a program's main route become abundantly clear in programs containing more than one conditional branch. Although the illustrations on previous pages focused on the ramifications of a single conditional branch statement, the schematic drawings here more accurately represent the structure of real-world programs, which may feature conditional branches as frequently as every five to eight steps. Were a VLIW compiler not able to advance selected instructions based on an analysis of the program's most likely path, instruction words would contain numerous blanks, and the opportunities for parallel execution by functional units would be held to a minimum.

Multiple branches—each a possible exit from the main trace—vastly complicate the work of the VLIW compiler, which must continually test and check its scheduling of instructions not only for the main trace but also for each of the other possible pathways the program may follow. The compiler program itself thus requires a great deal of memory to store the many rules it must apply. But since a single compiled

program is typically run over and over again, the investment of time and effort in a compiler that will ensure problem-free executions is well worth it.

These illustrations demonstrate the efficiency of VLIW compiling. The ninety instructions in the sequential program at far left have been compressed into twenty very long instruction words, arranged in blocks according to the branches with which they are associated. Arrows in the diagram below show how the program jumps from the main trace at the top to subsidiary traces and back again. But most of the processing action will take place in the main trace, tightly packed with instructions to maximize opportunities for parallelism.

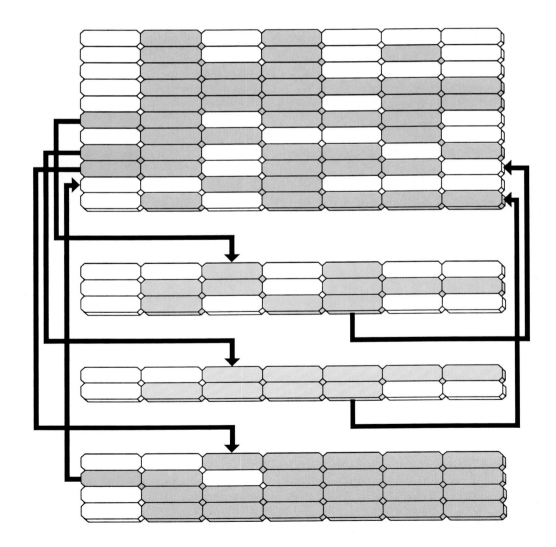

Glossary

Address: the numbered location of a specific cell in a computer's memory.

Algorithm: a step-by-step procedure for solving a problem; programming languages are essentially means of expressing algorithms.

Artificial intelligence (AI): the branch of computer science that attempts to create programs capable of emulating such human characteristics as learning and reasoning.

Assembler: a program that converts the mnemonic instructions of assembly-language programs into the zeros and ones of binary machine code.

Assembly language: a form of notation, specific to a given computer, in which a short mnemonic directly represents a specific instruction to the machine.

Binary code: a system for representing information by combinations of two symbols, such as ones and zeros.

Bit: the smallest unit of information in a digital computer, equivalent to a single zero or one. The word "bit" is a contraction of "binary digit."

Bug: an error that can cause software to fail.

Byte: a sequence of bits treated as a unit for computation or storage.

CASE (Computer-Aided Software Engineering): the use of a computer to help design and implement software systems. *See also* Software engineering.

Central processing unit (CPU): the part of the computer that interprets and executes instructions. It is composed of an arithmetic logic unit, a control unit, and a small amount of memory.

Class: a template for creating new objects in an object-oriented programming language. Objects of the same class have a common set of possible operations and, therefore, behave in a uniform fashion.

Code: one or more computer programs, or parts of computer programs.

Compatibility: the ability of two or more systems to exchange information.

Compiler: a program that converts a program written in a high-level language into either machine code or assembly language, holding the instructions in memory without executing them; the compiled program is stored for use at any later time.

Core memory: a type of computer memory that stores data on tiny magnetized rings suspended in a grid of current-carrying wires.

Data: a representation of facts, concepts, or instructions in a manner suitable for processing by computers.

Database: a collection of facts about a particular subject or related subjects organized in such a way as to be easily accessible to computer users.

Data dictionary: a collection of all the items of data used in a particular software system.

Debugging: the process of locating, analyzing, and correcting faults in a software system.

Disk: a round plate, generally made of plastic, metal, or glass, used for storing data either magnetically or optically.

Dynamic analysis: evaluating a program step by step as it runs.

Floating-point notation: a method of expressing numbers as the product of a fraction and a base number raised to a power; so named because the decimal point moves, or floats, depending on the size of the exponent. For instance, 93,000,000 can become either 0.93×10^8 or 0.093×10^9.

FORTRAN: a computer language used primarily for scientific or algebraic purposes.

Hard disk: a rigid metallic plate coated on both sides with a thin layer of magnetic material, where digital data is stored internally in the computer.

Hardware: the physical apparatus of a computer system.

High-level language: a programming language that approximates human language more closely than does machine code or assembly language, and in which one statement may invoke several machine-code or assembly-language instructions.

Input: information fed into a computer.

Instruction: an elementary machine-code or assembly-language order to a computer's central processing unit specifying an operation to be carried out by the computer; a sequence of instructions forms a program.

Interpreter: a program that translates a program written in a high-level language into machine code one line at a time, waits for the computer to perform the specified instructions, and then goes on to the next line.

List-processing language: a type of programming language that represents data as lists of words and other symbols in order to link concepts in a manner roughly analogous to the way they may be linked in the human brain.

Loop: a technique that allows a program to repeat a series of instructions a number of times.

Machine code: a set of binary digits that can be directly understood by a computer without translation.

Memory: the principal work space inside a computer in which data can be recorded or from which it is retrieved; the term applies to internal storage facilities as opposed to external storage, such as disks or tape.

Module: a discrete, separable portion of a program.

Monte Carlo method: a procedure that uses random sampling in order to approximate the solution of a problem; the Monte Carlo method is employed when the problem is too complex for a mathematical solution.

Object-oriented language: a type of programming language that builds software in units, or modules, called objects, each containing data and a set of operations to manipulate that data.

Operating system: a set of programs used to control, assist, or supervise all other programs that run on a computer system.

Output: the result of a computation, presented by a computer to the user, to another computer, or to some form of storage.

Parallel processing: computer processing technology that allows multiple operations to be performed at the same time.

Peripheral: a device that is attached to a computer; it includes all input or output devices and data-storage devices.

Program: a sequence of instructions for performing some operation or solving some problem by computer.

Programming language: a set of words, letters, numerals, and abbreviated mnemonics, regulated by a specific syntax, used to describe a program to a computer.

Random-access memory (RAM): temporary internal memory whose contents can be altered by the CPU; sometimes called read-and-write memory.

Read-only memory (ROM): permanent internal memory containing data or operating instructions that cannot be altered.

Reusability: the degree to which software modules can be used for multiple applications.

Sequential processing: the standard method of executing a program on a conventional, von Neumann computer, in which instructions are processed in a step-by-step, one-instruction-after-another fashion.

Simulation: the representation of the behavior of a real system with a computer model.

Software: instructions, or programs, that enable a computer to do useful work; contrasted with hardware, or the actual computer apparatus.

Software engineering: a systematic approach to the development and maintenance of software that begins with analysis of the software's goals or purposes.

Software tool: a computer program used in the development, testing, or maintenance of another computer program.

Source code: the lines of programming in a high-level language that are fed to a compiler or interpreter to be translated into machine code or assembly language.

Specifications: the stated requirements of a system under development.

Static analysis: evaluating a program without running it.

Structured programming: a systematic approach to the creation of software; in particular, it calls for dividing programs into small, independent tasks.

Syntax: the rules for arranging words and symbols in a programming language in a manner that is understandable to the language's compiler or interpreter.

System design: the process of defining the necessary components to satisfy the specifications for a software system.

Time-sharing: the simultaneous use of a computer by more than one person.

Validation: evaluating and testing software to ensure that it meets the design specifications.

Variable: a declared element whose value may be changed during a program's execution.

Virus: one form of program written with the intent of disrupting or disabling other software or hardware systems.

Bibliography

Books

Abbott, David, ed., *Mathematicians*. New York: Peter Bedrick Books, 1985.

American Men and Women of Science, edited by the Jaques Cattell Press. New York: R. R. Bowker Company, 1976.

Belzer, Jack, Albert G. Holzman, and Allen Kent, eds., "Project Mac." In *Encyclopedia of Computer Science and Technology*, Vol. 12. New York: Marcel Dekker Inc., 1979.

Brooks, Frederick P., Jr., *The Mythical Man-Month: Essays on Software Engineering*. Reading, Massachusetts: Addison-Wesley Publishing Company, 1975.

The CASE Experience, Annual CASE Survey 1988. Bellevue, Washington: CASE Research Corporation, 1988.

Computer Languages, by the Editors of Time-Life Books (Understanding Computers series). Alexandria, Virginia: Time-Life Books, 1986.

Corbató, F. J., Majorie Merwin-Daggett, and Robert C. Daley, "An Experimental Time-Sharing System." In *Programming Systems and Languages*, ed. by Saul Rosen. New York: McGraw-Hill Book Company, 1967.

Ditlea, Steve, ed., *Digital Deli*. New York: Workman Publishing, 1984.

Goldberg, Adele, *Smalltalk-80: The Interactive Programming Environment*. Reading, Massachusetts: Addison-Wesley Publishing Company, 1984.

Goldberg, Adele, and David Robson. *Smalltalk-80: The Language and Its Implementation*. Reading, Massachusetts: Addison-Wesley Publishing Company, 1983.

Hwang, Kai, and Fayé Briggs, *Computer Architecture and Parallel Processing*. New York: McGraw-Hill Book Company, 1984.

Input/Output, by the Editors of Time-Life Books (Understanding Computers series). Alexandria, Virginia: Time-Life Books, 1986.

Jones, Capers, *Programming Productivity*. New York: McGraw-Hill Book Company, 1986.

Kendall, Kenneth E., and Julie B. Kendall, *Systems Analysis and Design*. Englewood Cliffs, New Jersey: Prentice-Hall, Inc., 1988.

Letwin, Gordon, *Inside OS/2*. Redmond, Washington: Microsoft Press, 1988.

Marca, David A., and Clement L. McGowan, *SADT: Structured Analysis and Design Technique*. New York: McGraw-Hill Book Company, 1988.

Mitrani, I., *Simulation Techniques for Discrete Event Systems*. Cambridge: Cambridge University Press, 1982.

Peterson, Gerald E., *Tutorial: Object-Oriented Computing*, Vol. 1: Concepts. Washington, D.C.: Computer Society Press of the IEEE, 1987.

Pugh, Emerson W., *Memories That Shaped an Industry*. Cambridge, Massachusetts: The MIT Press, 1984.

Ralston, Anthony, and Edwin D. Reilly, Jr., eds., *Encyclopedia of Computer Science and Engineering*, 2d edition. New York: Van Nostrand Reinhold Company, 1983.

Skwirzynski, Jozef K., ed., *Software System Design Methods: The Challenge of Advanced Computing Technology*. Berlin: Springer-Verlag, 1986.

Streitmatter, Gene A., *Software: Programming Concepts and Techniques*. Reston, Virginia: Reston Publishing Company, Inc., 1981.

Vick, C. R., and C. V. Ramamoorthy, eds., *Handbook of Software Engineering*. New York: Van Nostrand Reinhold Company, no date.

Wexelblat, Richard L., ed., *History of Programming Languages*. New York: Academic Press, 1981.

Yourdon, Edward:

Classics in Software Engineering. New York: Yourdon Press, 1979.

Managing the Structured Techniques. Englewood Cliffs, New Jersey: Prentice-Hall, Inc., 1979.

Periodicals

Alper, Alan, "Odd Couple: Tarkenton, Martin Merge to Automate Software." *Computerworld*, September 22, 1986.

Althoff, James C., Jr., "Building Data Structures in the Smalltalk-80 System." *BYTE*, August 1981.

Aron, Joel D., Frederick P. Brooks, Jr., Bob O. Evans, John W. Fairclough, Aaron Finerman, Bernard A. Galler, William P. Heising, Walter H. Johnson, and Nancy Stern, "Discussion of the SPREAD Report." *Annals of the History of Computing*, January 1983.

Bachman, Charlie, "A CASE for Reverse Engineering." *Datamation*, July 1, 1988.

Backus, John:

"Can Programming Be Liberated from the von Neumann Style? A Functional Style and Its Algebra of Programs." *Communications of the ACM*, August 1978.

"Function-Level Computing." *IEEE Spectrum*, August 1982.

Betz, David, "An XLISP Tutorial." *BYTE*, March 1985.

Boehm, Barry W., "Improving Software Productivity." *Computer*, September 1987.

Bouldin, Barbara, "Implementing CASE: From Strategy to Reality." *Computerworld*, November 9, 1987.

Brooks, Frederick P., Jr., "No Silver Bullet: Essence and Accidents of Software Engineering." *IEEE Computer*, April 1987.

Brooks, Geraldine, "Faced with a Changing Work Force, TRW Pushes to Raise White-Collar Productivity." *Wall Street Journal*, September 22, 1983.

Chapnick, Philip, "CASE in Point." *Database Programming & Design*, October 1988.

Connor, Albert J., and Albert F. Case, Jr., "Making a Case for CASE." *Computerworld*, July 9, 1986.

Corbató, F. J., "PL/1 as a Tool for System Programming." *Datamation*, May 1969.

Cox, Brad, and Bill Hunt, "Objects, Icons, and Software-ICs." *BYTE,* August 1986.

Cunningham, Ward, and Kent Beck, "Diagramming Objects." *AI Expert,* November 1987.

Currie, Edward H., "The Only Good Bug Is a Dead Bug." *Computer Language,* February 1987.

Dahl, Ole-Johan, and Kristen Nygaard, "SIMULA—An Algol-Based Simulation Language." *Communications of the ACM,* September 1966.

"The Datamation Hall of Fame." *Datamation,* September 15, 1987.

Deutsch, L. Peter, "Building Control Structures in the Smalltalk-80 System." *BYTE,* August 1981.

Duff, Charles B., "Designing an Efficient Language." *BYTE,* August 1986.

Endres, Tim, "Clascal—An Object-Oriented Pascal." *Computer Language,* May 1985.

Evans, Bob O., "System/360: A Retrospective View." *Annals of the History of Computing,* April 1986.

Feder, Barnaby J., "Computer Helper: Software Tat Writes Software." *The New York Times,* May 8, 1988.

Fisher, David A., "DoD's Common Programming Language Effort." *IEEE Computer,* March 1978.

Forman, Fred L., and Jerrold M. Grochow:
"Getting Productivity from Productivity Tools." *Computing Canada,* May 28, 1987.
"New Tools, Old Approach." *Computerworld,* September 7, 1987.

Gelernter, David, "Programming for Advanced Computing." *Scientific American,* October 1987.

Glaser, E. L., and F. J. Corbató, "Introduction to Time-Sharing." *Datamation,* November 1964.

Goldberg, Adele, "Introducing the Smalltalk-80 System." *BYTE,* August 1981.

Gries, David, Raymond Miller, Robert Ritchie, and Paul Young, "Imbalance between Growth and Funding in Academic Computing Science: Two Trends Colliding." *Communications of the ACM,* September 1986.

Grochow, Jerrold M., "CASE Pilot Caution Urged." *Computerworld,* November 16, 1987.

Haanstra, John W., Bob O. Evans, Joel D. Aron, Frederick P. Brooks, Jr., John W. Fairclough, William P. Heising, Herbert Hellerman, Walter H. Johnson, Michael J. Kelly, Douglas V. Newton, Bruce G. Oldfield, Seymour A. Rosen, and Jerrold Svigals, "Processor Products—Final Report of SPREAD Task Group, December 28, 1961." *Annals of the History of Computing,* January 1983.

Hayes, Brian, "Scissors, Paper, Stone: A Tournament of Schemes." *Computer Language,* December 1986.

Heller, Martin, "An Architecture for the Future." *PC Tech Journal,* November 1987.

Hellerman, Herbert, Robert W. O'Neill, Gene M. Amdahl, and

Jerome Svigals, "The SPREAD Discussion Continued." *Annals of the History of Computing,* April 1984.

Humphrey, Watts S., "Characterizing the Software Process: A Maturity Framework." *IEEE Software,* March 1988.

Ingalls, Daniel H.:
"Design Principles behind Smalltalk." *BYTE,* August 1981.
"The Smalltalk Graphics Kernel." *BYTE,* August 1981.

Janus, Susan, "CASE Tools Aid in Complex Software Design." *PC Week,* April 19, 1988.

Jones, T. Capers, "Reusability in Programming: A Survey of the State of the Art." *IEEE Tutorial: Software Reusability,* 1986.

Joyce, Edward J., "Reusable Software: Passage to Productivity?" *Datamation,* September 15, 1988.

Kull, David, "The Rough Road to Productivity." *Computer Decisions,* February 23, 1987.

Leibowitz, Martin A., "Queues." *Scientific American,* August 1968.

McGregor, John D., "Object-Oriented Programming with SCOOPS." *Computer Language,* July 1987.

Machrone, Bill, "The 80386: The More Things Change. . ." *PC Magazine,* June 24, 1986.

Manuel, Tom, "Special Report: Integration Is Crucial to CASE's Future." *Electronics,* September 17, 1987.

Mealy, G. H., "The Functional Structure of OS/360." *IBM Systems Journal,* Vol. 5, No. 1, 1966.

Miller, Harry, "The Future through Windows." *PC World,* April 1987.

Minasi, Mark, "Why OS/2?" *BYTE,* August 1988.

Nygaard, Kristen, "Basic Concepts in Object Oriented Programming." *SIGPLAN Notices,* October 1986.

O'Donnell, John, "A Fine-Grained, High-Performance Alternative." *Computer Design,* June 1, 1987.

Parnas, David Lorge, "Software Aspects of Strategic Defense Systems." *Communications of the ACM,* December 1985.

Parrello, Bruce D., Waldo C. Kabat, and L. Wos, "Job-Shop Scheduling Using Automated Reasoning: A Case Study of the Car-Sequencing Problem." *Journal of Automated Reasoning,* Vol. 2, 1986.

Pascoe, Geoffrey A., "Elements of Object-Oriented Programming." *BYTE,* August 1986.

Patrick, Robert L., "The Seed of Empire." *Datamation,* May 15, 1984.

Petzold, Charles:
"Exploring the OS/2 Video Interface." *PC Magazine,* December 22, 1987.
"Getting the OS/2 Threads in Hand." *PC Magazine,* March 15, 1988.
"OS/2 Kernel Programming." *PC Magazine,* November 10, 1987.
"OS/2—Ready to Take on DOS—Has a Familiar Feel." *PC Magazine,* January 26, 1988.

Port, Otis, John W. Verity, Anne R. Field, Susan M. Gelford, and

Keith H. Hammonds, "The Software Trap: Automate—Or Else." *Business Week,* May 9, 1988.

Pountain, Dick, "Object-Oriented FORTH." *BYTE,* August 1986.

Quedens, Guy, "Windows Virtual Machine." *PC Tech Journal,* October 1987.

Quedens, Guy, and Steven Armbrust, "Windows Memory Management." *PC Tech Journal,* October 1987.

Ramamoorthy, C. V., and Farokh B. Bastani, "Software Reliability—Status and Perspectives." *IEEE Transactions on Software Engineering,* July 1982.

Rasmussen, E. Hart, "Queue Simulation." *BYTE,* March 1984.

Rifkin, Glenn, "James Martin's Show Goes On." *Computerworld,* November 9, 1987.

Robson, David, "Object-Oriented Software Systems." *BYTE,* August 1981.

Schindler, Max:
"Advanced Tools Finally Start to Automate Software Design." *Electronic Design,* November 27, 1987.
"Software Development Parallels Computer Hardware Advances." *Electronic Design,* February 4, 1988.

Schmucker, Kurt J., "Object-Oriented Languages for the Macintosh." *BYTE,* August 1986.

Serlin, Omri, "Multiflow Takes a Radical Approach to High Speed Computing." *Unix/World,* August 1987.

Shapiro, Ezra, "Three New Spreadsheets." *BYTE,* November 1987.

Silverman, Barry G., "Software Cost and Productivity Improvements: An Analogical View." *IEEE Computer,* May 1985.

Simon, Stephen D., "To Err Isn't Only Human." *Computer Language,* March 1986.

Smith, Robert S., "The 1024-Bit Word." *Government Data Systems,* October 1987.

Snyders, Jan, "A CASE of Unknown Identity." *Infosystems,* October 1987.

"Something Rotten in the State of Software." *The Economist,* January 9, 1988.

Stamps, David, "CASE: Cranking Out Productivity." *Datamation,* July 1, 1987.

Stern, Hal L., "Comparison of Window Systems." *BYTE,* November 1987.

Strehlo, Kevin, "Small Talk with Alan Kay." *Computer Language,* January 1986.

Stroustrup, Bjarne, "What is Object-Oriented Programming." *IEEE Software,* May 1988.

Tazelaar, Jane Morrill, "In Depth Multitasking." *BYTE,* July 1988.

Tello, Ernest R., "Object-Oriented Programming." *Dr. Dobb's Journal,* March 1987.

Tesler, Lawrence G.:
"Programming Experiences." *BYTE,* August 1986.
"Programming Languages." *Scientific American,* September 1984.

"The Smalltalk Environment." *BYTE,* August 1981.

Tucker, S. G., "Microprogram Control for System/360." *IBM Systems Journal,* Vol. 6, No. 4, 1967.

Ungar, David, and David Patterson, "What Price Smalltalk?" *IEEE Computer,* January 1987.

Vaughan, Kristi, "Multiflow Hopes Its Super Computers Mean Super Growth." *Business Digest of Greater New Haven,* January 1988.

Voelcker, John, "Software: Common Interfaces/Expert Systems." *IEEE Spectrum,* January 1988.

Von Simson, Charles, "AT&T Readies Itself for a Sea Change." *Information Week,* September 19, 1988.

Watson, Thomas J., Jr., "The Greatest Capitalist in History." *Fortune,* August 31, 1987.

Wegner, Peter, "Dimensions of Object-Based Language Design." *OOPSLA'87 Proceedings,* October 4-7, 1987.

Williamson, Mickey, "Case by Case." *CIO Magazine,* April 1988.

Winograd, Terry, "Beyond Programming Languages." *Communications of the ACM,* July 1979.

Wise, T. A.:
"IBM's $5,000,000,000 Gamble." *Fortune,* September 1966.
"The Rocky Road to the Marketplace." *Fortune,* October 1966.

Wolfe, Alexander, "Software Productivity Moves Upstream." *Electronics,* July 10, 1986.

Wolfe, Alexander, and Jonah McLeod, "Emerging Computer Tools Speed Up Software Design." *Electronics,* July 24, 1986.

The Xerox Learning Research Group, "The Smalltalk-80 System." *BYTE,* August 1981.

Yourdon, Edward:
"The Economics of CASE: Present and Future." *American Programmer,* October 1988.
"The Emergence of Structured Analysis." *Computer Decisions,* April 1976.

Other Sources

Albrecht, Allan J., "Measuring Application Development Productivity." Proceedings, Application Development Symposium, Monterey, California, October 14-17, 1979.

"Bachman Company Backgrounder." Company literature. Cambridge, Massachusetts: Bachman Information Systems, 1988.

"California Utility Reaches 'Watershed' in Software System Development." Company literature. Waltham, Massachusetts: Cortex Corporation, 1988.

Chan, P. Y., *Stochastic Treatment of the Failure Rate in Software Reliability Growth Models.* London: Centre for Software Reliability, 1986.

Colwell, Robert P., Robert P. Nix, John J. O'Donnell, David B. Papworth, and Paul K. Rodman, *A VLIW Architecture for a Trace Scheduling Compiler.* Branford, Connecticut:

Multiflow Computer, Inc., 1987.

Corbató, F. J., and C. T. Clingen, "A Managerial View of the Multics System Development." Under Authority of Advanced Research Projects Agency of the Department of Defense, no date.

Corbató, F. J., C. T. Clingen, and J. H. Saltzer, "Multics—The First Seven Years." *AFIPS Conference Proceedings,* spring 1972.

Corbató, F. J., and V. A. Vyssotsky, "Introduction and Overview of the Multics System," no date.

"Diagramming Tools of the Information Engineering Facility." Product literature. Plano, Texas: Texas Instruments, September 1987.

Fisher, Joseph A., *VLIW Architectures: Supercomputing via Overlapped Execution.* Branford, Connecticut: Multiflow Computer, Inc., 1987.

Howden, William E., "Program Testing versus Proofs of Correctness." *Technical Report Number CS88-121.* San Diego: University of California, February 1988.

Lubeck, Olaf M., *Supercomputer Performance: The Theory, Practice, and Results.* Los Alamos National Laboratory, January 1988.

Martin, James, and E. A. Hershey III, "Information Engineering: A Management White Paper." Company literature. Atlanta, Georgia: KnowledgeWare, Inc., 1986.

Meyrowitz, Norman, ed., *Object-Oriented Programming Systems, Languages and Applications.* Proceedings of a Conference October 4-8, 1987, Orlando, Florida. Published as *SIGPLAN Notices,* Vol. 22, No. 12, December 1987.

"NeXT Product Information." NeXT Inc., 1988.

Passmore, Phil L., "Bermuda—Birthplace of CASE Technology." Unpublished manuscript. New York, 1987.

Serlin, Omri, ed., *The Serlin Report on Parallel Processing.* December 4, 1987.

Software Reliability. Maidenhead Berkshire, England: Pergamon Infotech Limited, 1986.

Technical Summary. Branford, Connecticut: Multiflow Computer, Inc., June 23, 1987.

Acknowledgments

The editors wish to thank the following individuals and institutions for their help in the preparation of this volume: **In the United States**: California—San Francisco: Edward F. Miller, Jr., Software Research Inc.; San Jose: John Backus, IBM; Santa Monica: Barry Boehm; Palo Alto: L. Peter Deutsch and Adele Goldberg, ParcPlace Systems; Connecticut—Branford: Joseph Fisher, Aeleen Frish, and John O'Donnell, MULTIFLOW Computer, Inc.; New Haven: Paul Hudak, Yale University; Georgia—Atlanta: Kim Addington, Knowledge-Ware, Inc.; Louisiana—Baton Rouge: Peter Chen, Chen and Associates, Inc.; Maryland—Bethesda: Anthony Jordano, IBM Federal Systems; College Park: John Gannon, University of Maryland; Kensington: Jane Gruenebaum; Michigan—Southfield: Tom Stanton, Nastec Corporation; Minnesota—Northfield: Brian Hayes; New Jersey—Morris Plains: James B. Webber, OMICRON; Piscataway: Duane Luse, AT&T; New York—Albany: Isabel Nirenberg, State University of New York; New York: Edward Yourdon; North Carolina—Chapel Hill: Frederick P. Brooks, Jr., University of North Carolina; Ohio—Cleveland: Frank Smith, Ernst & Whinney; Rhode Island—Providence: Peter Wegner, Brown University; Texas—Plano: Dale Dukes, Texas Instruments; Virginia—Arlington: Jerrold Grochow, American Management Systems, Inc.; Reston: Walter S. Key; Arthur B. Pyster, Software Productivity Consortium; Washington—Bellevue: Greg Boone, CASE Research Corporation; Redmond: Russell Werner, Microsoft Corporation.

Picture Credits

Index

*Numerals in italics indicate an illustration
of the subject mentioned.*

Monte Carlo techniques: 102
Multics (Multiplexed Information and Computing Service): 34-36
Multitasking: *92-97*

N
Nastec Corporation: 62
Newell, Allen: 89
Nichols, Herman: 51
Norwegian Computer Center (NCC): 102, 103
Norwegian Defense Research Establishment (NDRE): 102
N-version programming: 16
Nygaard, Kristen: 102-103, 104, 106

O
Objective C: 89, 105
Object-oriented programming: 71, *72-83*, 89-90, 101-106; and Smalltalk, 101, 103-104
Object Pascal: 105
Operating systems: 26; Multics, 34-36; OS/360, 26-27, 30-34

P
Parallelizing compilers: 10*7*, *109-117*
Parallel processing: and new languages, 87, 89, 100
Parnas, David L.: 37, 38
Pascal: 20, 36
PL/1 (Programming Language One): 27, 35
Programmers: number, 20
Programming: computer-aided, 39, *40-49*, 51, 57, 62, 64-70; and manpower, 32; productivity enhancement in coding, 51, 54-57; productivity enhancement in design, 57, 60-63; productivity measurement, 52, 53, 54; steps, 21;

and time-sharing, 36. *See also* CASE; Languages; Systems programming; Validation

Q
Quicksort: 22

R
Raytheon Corporation: ReadyCode, 56

S
SABRE: 64
SDI (Strategic Defense Initiative): distributed systems and software, 36-38
Simula: 20, 89, 102-103; Simula 67, 103-104
Simulations: with object-oriented programs, 71, *72-83*, 103
Smalltalk: 20, 89, 101; development, 104-105; Smalltalk 80, 105
Software: 19; compatibility with hardware, 26; complexity measurement, 53-54; engineering, 60; industry, 20-21; library of modules, 55; logical inconsistencies, 6-7, *28-29*; for parallel processors, 107; rate of production, 19-20, 51-52. *See also* Programming; Validation
Special cases: testing, *10-11*
Sperry Rand: 21
Sposato, Steve: 56
SPREAD (Systems Programming, Research, Engineering, and Development): 24-26
State-based analysis: *See* CASE
Structured analysis: 60-61
Structured programming: 60, 98-99
Systems analysis: 39, 57; process-oriented, 62-63
Systems programming: 22, 23; organizing,

31-33; System/360 development, 23-27, 30-34
System/360: history, 23-27, 30-34

T
Tarkington, Fran: 64
Tarkington Software, Inc.: 64
Texas Instruments: Information Engineering Facility, 64
Time-sharing: and Multics, 34-36
Traces: and parallelizing compilers, 110, *112-117*
TRW: 54-55
Turing, Alan M.: Turing Award, 85

U
UNIVAC 1107: 103

V
Validation: entire program, *16-17*; functional testing, 7, *8-11*; structural testing, 7, *12-15*
Virusafe: 59
Viruses: *58-59*
VLIW (very long instruction word): 107; compilers, *108-117*
Von Neumann, John: 88

W
Watson, Thomas J.: 23, 24, 33
Webber, Jim: 54, 57, 67
Williams, Al: 30
Windows: *92-97*

X
Xerox: PARC (Palo Alto Research Center), 104

Y
Yourdon, Edward: 60

THE CONSULTANTS

BARRY W. BOEHM, chief scientist in the Office of Technology for the TRW Defense Systems Group in Redondo Beach, California, is responsible for the Group's Ada office and Quantum Leap, a program to improve productivity in software development at TRW. An adjunct professor of computer science at the University of California at Los Angeles, he has been recognized by the computer science community through several awards and honors.

LEIGH D. CAGAN is the director of Marketing and Technical Communications for MULTIFLOW Computer, Inc., in Branford, Connecticut.

CHRISTOPHER K. CARLSON, assistant professor of decision sciences at George Mason University, specializes in information-resource management. His research is in decision support and expert systems.

JAMES H. DOBBINS is the director of Software Quality Engineering for American Management Systems, Inc., in Arlington, Virginia.

JOHN D. GANNON, professor in the Department of Computer Sciences at the University of Maryland, does research in software engineering and programming languages.

BRIAN HAYES has written about computers and computing for *Scientific American, BYTE,* and *Computer Language.* He is author of a book about Scheme, a dialect of the LISP programming language.

MARK MACKAMAN is the OS/2 product marketing manager at Microsoft Corporation in Redmond, Washington.

JAMES WEBBER is president of Omicron, the Center for Information Technology Management, in Mountain Lakes, New Jersey. Omicron is a membership organization of senior information-systems professionals in major corporations.

PETER WEGNER, a professor of computer science at Brown University, has taught computer science at the London School of Economics, Pennsylvania State University, and Cornell University. He has written numerous books and papers on various topics in computer science and pursues research in object-oriented, functional, database, and distributed approaches to programming.

DAVID R. WILSON is the national director of Information Systems Consulting Services for Ernst and Whinney in Cleveland, Ohio. An expert on computer security, he also directs Ernst and Whinney's Information Security Services Practice.

Library of Congress Cataloging in Publication Data

The Software Challenge / by the editors of Time-Life Books, Inc.
p.   cm.—(Understanding computers)
Bibliography: p.
Includes index.
ISBN 0-8094-6058-0
1. Computer software.   2. Computer software industry.
I. Time-Life Books.   II. Series.
QA76.754.S646 1989   338.4'70053—dc19   88-29546
CIP

ISBN 0-8094-6059-9 (lib.bdg.)

For information on and a full description of any of the Time-Life Books series listed, please call 1-800-621-7026 or write:
Reader Information
Time-Life Customer Service
P.O. Box C-32068
Richmond, Virginia 23261-2068